W9-CES-975

WITHDRAWN

IS MY CHURCH WHAT GOD MEANT IT TO BE?

Gary L. Hauck

LIBRARY
BRYAN COLLEGE
DAYTON, TN. 37321

ACCENT BOOKS
Denver, Colorado

64256

MEMBER OF
EVANGELICAL CHRISTIAN
PUBLISHERS ASSOCIATION

Except where otherwise indicated, Scripture quotations are from the New American Standard Bible, ©The Lockman Foundation 1960, 1962, 1963, 1968, 1971, 1972, 1973, 1975, and are used by permission.

Scripture verses marked AV are from the Authorized Version.

Much of the material in this book was completed as a project for Dallas Theological Seminary and is used here, with revisions, by permission.

ACCENT BOOKS
A division of Accent-B/P Publications, Inc.
12100 W. Sixth Avenue
P.O. Box 15337
Denver, Colorado 80215

Copyright © 1979 Accent-B/P Publications, Inc.
Printed in United States of America

All rights reserved. No portion of this book may be reproduced in any form without the written permission of the publishers, with the exception of brief excerpts in magazine reviews.

Library of Congress Catalog Card Number: 79-50811

ISBN 0-89636-029-6

*Dedicated to
my wife Lois
whose sense of balance in life
is a constant challenge to me*

FOREWORD

Balance between extremes in the local church has always been hard to attain and to maintain. It is still so today. Not compromise, but balance that is biblical—that is what the author of this volume rightly calls for. His chief concern, as the title indicates, is with the New Testament teaching of the local church. This study touches all the essential areas of the function and ministry of the local church.

Mr. Hauck writes with the firm conviction that the local church is the divine institution through which God's work is to be carried out. He seeks to present the New Testament as the criterion by which every concept regarding the form and function of the local church is to be judged. The views embraced in this study are presented carefully and clearly. The call is for commitment to biblical balance in the work and worship of the local assembly.

Robert P. Lightner
Dallas Theological Seminary

CONTENTS

INTRODUCTION

The Stained Glass Pendulum

Throughout the history of the church, the evangelical assembly has been perennially challenged by the perplexity of the pendulum—that is, the tendency to lean toward extremes. This generation is no different. Subtle polarizations occur among the most sincere laypeople and leaders of the church, who are usually unaware of it. Such extremism, however, leads to an unhealthy functioning of the local body of believers and is a poor testimony to the surrounding unbelieving society.

I will never forget the words of the pastor who discipled me in the ministry. He would say the same phrase over and over and over again. I could hear him say it in my sleep: "Gary, the key word in the ministry is *balance!*" This is one of the most significant principles that I have ever heard concerning the ministry.

One day, we are told, a young servant of Christ asked D. L. Moody, "Sir, which is more important to a Christian—prayer or Bible reading?" Without hesitation, the wise preacher responded by asking a question, "Young man, which is more important to a bird—his right wing or his left?" That was a discerning insight into the importance of balance!

But where should today's local church go in search of the vital principles pertaining to balance? The answer ought to be obvious to every Bible-believing evangelical, for all questions concerning the life of the church must logically be directed to the Head of the Church, the Chief Shepherd—the Lord Jesus Christ—and His Word.

It is the purpose of this project to attempt to identify some of the subtle temptations to unhealthy imbalance in the local church, and then see what divine principles are set forth by the Chief Shepherd and His Word in directing us toward biblical balance.

Since biblical information necessitates application (cf. James 1:22), an important feature of this manual will be the applicational projects at the end of each chapter. Whether you are a local church leader or a layperson, you have the exciting challenge of putting these principles into shoe leather.

While in no way denying the doctrine of the universal church, this discussion will be limited to the visible and functional expression of the local church.

What is a local church? I like the definition of Paul R. Jackson:

A local New Testament church is a body of believers immersed upon a credible confession of faith in Jesus Christ, having two officers (pastors [elders] and deacons), sovereign in polity, and banded together for work, worship, the observance of the ordinances and the worldwide proclamation of the gospel.[1]

It is upon this definition that my thoughts are based.

1
Balancing
the Purpose

THE SWING OF THE PENDULUM

Everglow Evangelistic Church cannot contain its super growth. Its bright red buses permeate the community. Last Sunday two thousand attended to see Reverend Reacher swallow a live goldfish. Forty walked the aisle after his gospel message. Praise the Lord! But there is some rumbling at the water fountain.

"Deacon Do-Good?" earnest Ernie asked searchingly.

"Yes, my friend, what can I do for you?"

"I'm a little frustrated," confessed the young inquirer. "I've come to this church for five years now—five years. I love the pastor, and I love seeing people getting saved. But . . . ah . . . "

"Yes? But what?" returned the deacon.

"I don't know. Maybe it's just me, but . . . as I look back over the past five years, I haven't seen much of a change in me. I'm still fighting the same spiritual conflicts. My wife and I are still toughing it out, but it can't go on much longer. She and I haven't matured much. I'd love to be a spiritual leader, learn the Word of God and be able to apply it to my life, but I just don't seem to get any teaching here."

Deacon Do-Good looked perplexed. "Haven't you been listening to the evangelistic preaching here for the last five years?"

Ernie let the conversation end.

The following week earnest Ernie visited the Diehard Doctrine Fellowship. What a refreshing change! The organist ended the Bach chorale, and that was the cue. Out came the black notebooks. Every one of the twenty-four members opened their underlined Bibles with eager anticipation.

"The first word in verse six," Dr. Teacher explained, "is crucial in understanding this entire passage." Ernie was finally being taught.

After the service, Ernie smiled at the tall, slender man sitting next to him in the pew. "I'm a visitor. Is this your regular attendance?" he asked cordially.

"Amen!" came the proud response. "We've been able to hold her at twenty-four for the past three years! And we have matured deeply in the faith."

Ernie's sparkle faded. He went home and looked under "churches" in the Yellow Pages, but alas—he found these were the only two Bible-believing churches in his community.

Ernie was in a dilemma. He could join a fellowship which was growing in quantity but not in quality, or he could join a fellowship which was growing in quality but not in quantity.

Ernie's dilemma uncovers a major tension in current church thought, the tension of *purpose*. What is the purpose of the local church? To the Everglow Evangelistic Church, the purpose is obviously evangelism. To the Diehard Doctrine Fellowship, the purpose is obviously edification through biblical education.

Both views in themselves are commendable. The difficulty, however, is that those who stress evangelism do so, too often, at the expense or exclusion of biblical education and edification. On the other hand, those who stress biblical education and edification do so, too often, at the expense or exclusion of evangelism.

What is the answer to Ernie's dilemma? The leaders of the church must know the *biblical* purpose of the church. Alvin J. Lindgren defines church administration as, " . . . the task of discovering and clarifying the goals and purpose of the field it serves and of moving in a coherent, comprehensive manner toward their realization."[1]

WHAT DID JESUS SAY?

Jesus said, "Go therefore and *make disciples* of all the nations, baptizing them in the name of the Father and the Son and the Holy Spirit, *teaching* them to observe all that I commanded you . . . " (Matthew 28:19-20; emphasis mine).

FURTHER BIBLICAL INSTRUCTION

The Apostle Paul later said:

And He gave some as apostles, and some as prophets, and some as evangelists, and some as pastors and teachers, for the equipping of the saints for the work of service, to the building up of the body of Christ; until we all attain to the unity of the faith, and of the knowledge of the Son of God, to a mature man, to the measure of the stature which belongs to the fulness of Christ. As a result, we are no longer to be children, tossed here and there by waves, and carried about by every wind of doctrine, by the trickery of men, by craftiness in deceitful scheming; but speaking the truth in love, we are to grow up in all aspects into Him, who is the head, even Christ, from whom the whole body, being fitted and held together by that which every joint supplies, according to the proper working of each individual part, causes the growth of the body for the building up of itself in love (Ephesians 4:11-16).

SIGNIFICANT OBSERVATIONS

The Great Commission of Jesus Christ, as cited in Matthew 28:19-20, is perhaps the most quoted yet least observed verse in the Bible by men speaking of the purpose of the church. It is sad but true that many sincere evangelicals believe that the Great Commission consists of only one facet—evangelism. However, the careful observer will see that this commission actually includes three major facets or responsibilities. Evangelism is only one-third of it! Notice the three steps: "make disciples . . . baptizing them . . . teaching them." Actually, according to Philip R. Williams, "make disciples" is the only imperative while "baptizing" and "teaching" serve as circumstantial participles. However, the circumstantial participle of attendant circumstance "may express an idea which is not subordinate to the action of a finite verb . . . but is of equal force with the action of the finite verb."[2]

How interesting! Jesus Christ was equally concerned with *quantitative and qualitative* growth!

The Authorized Version translates two different words from the original into the same English word, "teach." The New American Standard Bible quoted above cor-

16

rectly renders the first word in verse 19, "make disciples" (which literally means "disciplize") and "teach" in verse 20, from a word meaning "to instruct."

The second step in the Great Commission was also of significant importance to Jesus, and included the identification of the converts to Jesus Christ and the church by the public testimony of water baptism.

So, the mandate of our Saviour may be summarized: (1) make disciples; (2) identify the disciples; and (3) lead the disciples into maturity by means of instruction.

In the Ephesians 4 passage, we see an implementation of the Great Commission. In verse 11, Paul lists the gifts of spiritual leadership and then explains their purpose in verse 12. Expressly stated, the Lord gave these gifts "for the equipping of the saints." But for what were the saints equipped? "For the work of service," is Paul's reply.

What is the nature of that service? Here is the explosive conclusion: "to the building up of the body of Christ." The body of Christ, of course, is the church. The original word for "build" is the Greek word, *oikodome,* which includes the meaning of quantity and quality—expansion and stabilization.

The significant contribution of this entire passage not only presents a balanced view of the purpose of the church, but also gives characteristics of the type of disciple which the local church is to develop:

1. *Productivity* (verse 12). The disciple is to be himself equipped "for the work of service, to the building up of the body of Christ."

2. *Unity* (verse 13). The disciple is to be in harmony with the doctrine of the Christian gospel held by his fellow believers. He will experience a oneness

with the rest of the body.

3. *Maturity* (verse 13). The disciple is to manifest spiritual maturity which is defined in this verse as Christlikeness.

4. *Stability* (verse 14). The disciple is to be stable in his position upon the Word of God—not easily swayed by "every wind of doctrine."

5. *Veracity* (verse 15). The disciple is to be characterized by truthfulness—especially as it relates to his sharing the truths of the Word of God.

6. *Charity* (verse 15). It is not enough for the disciple to speak the truth, for he must learn to do it "in love." Love is the mark of a truly mature disciple.

7. *Interdependability* (verse 16). The disciple must learn to function in the body by a mutual relationship of contribution and reception. He must be eager enough to expend himself for the brethren and remain humble enough to be, at the same time, a recipient of their spiritual contributions.

PUTTING IT INTO PARAPHRASE

Reviewing the Scriptures in light of the above observations, one could paraphrase the biblical perspective of the purpose of the church:

Going, therefore, make disciples of all the nations, publicly identifying them with Christ and the church in the waters of baptism, in the name of the Father and the Son and the Holy Spirit, leading them into spiritual maturity by instructing them in My word

(Matthew 28:19-20).

And He gave some Christians apostles; and some, prophets; and some, evangelists; and some, pastor-teachers; for the purpose of equipping the saints in order that they may be enabled to do the work of the ministry which involves the building up of the church of Christ both in quantity and quality, until all of us come into a place of believing true doctrine, knowing the Son of God in an intimate way, and maturing into Christlikeness; so that our minds and hearts will not be so unstable, docile, and pliable as they are now, making us susceptible to all kinds of incorrect doctrines; but that we might be able to speak the truth in love, and mature spiritually in Christ in every respect, and emulate Him, since He is the Head of the church.

Christ, Himself, is the One who designed His spiritual body, and carefully fitted every part together in just the way He desired, so that every part, in its way, may function healthily by contributing to the rest of the body that which will strengthen and edify itself in love (Ephesians 4:11-16).

THE QUESTION STATED

What, then, is the immediate goal of the local church? The biblical goal of the local church is the building up of the body of Christ both in quantity *and* quality to present to God believers who are both mature and spiritually reproductive. Why? The Westminster Confession states it well: "The chief end of man is to glorify God . . . " Our ultimate occupation in the building of Christ's church is the magnification of Almighty God.

PUTTING IT ALL TOGETHER

Balance is the key word concerning the purpose of the church. The local church must not emphasize evangelism at the expense of edification. At the same time, it must not emphasize edification at the expense of evangelism. Discipleship involves *both*. Lloyd Perry and Edward Lias have stated the caution well:

> We urge the pastor to recall his purposes from time to time, thus keeping sight of his goal. In coopera-tion with God and the congregation, the minister should aim to realize the goal of a born-again membership; a people devoted to prayer, interces-sion, thanksgiving and praise; a testifying, witness-ing membership which speaks in the boldness of the Spirit in the church, home, school, and shop. The membership should be devoted to a sacrifice of time, treasure and talents. Labor to achieve a membership which is Spirit-filled. Likewise, a Bible-centered and Bible-studying membership, given to daily Bible study and devotion. The pastor and people should become progressively missionary-minded, heeding the admonition, "go ye into all the world and preach the Gospel."[3]

APPLICATION PROJECT

For the Church Leader and Layperson

1. Circle the best answer: My church needs to be . . .
   a. more evangelistic.
   b. more concerned with edifying and educating our people in the Word of God.
2. List four specific ways your church could improve in this area:
   a. _____
   b. _____
   c. _____
   d. _____
3. True or false: I will complain about this area to other church members.
4. True or false: I will lovingly and prayerfully mention this area of need along with my four specific suggestions at the next appropriate leaders' meeting.
5. If your answer to #1 was letter "a," read through the Book of Acts in your personal devotional time this week. If your answer was "b," make a personal study of the Book of Ephesians.
6. In fifty words or less, write out your personal testimony as you would share it with a friend.
7. Begin memorizing Romans 3:23; 6:23; 5:8; 10:9,10,13 if you haven't already done so.
8. Prayerfully ponder the following story:

On a dangerous seacoast where shipwrecks often occur there was once a crude little lifesaving station. The building was just a hut, and there was only one boat, but the few devoted members kept a constant watch over the sea, and, with no thought for themselves, went out day and night tirelessly searching for the lost.

Many lives were saved by this wonderful little station, so it became famous. Some of those who were saved, and various others in the surrounding area, wanted to become associated with the station and give of their time, money and effort for the support of its work. New boats were bought and crews trained. The little lifesaving station grew.

Some of the new members of the lifesaving station were unhappy that the building was so crude and poorly equipped. They felt a more comfortable place should be provided . . . so they replaced the emergency cots and beds and put better furniture in the enlarged building. Now the lifesaving station became a popular gathering place . . . it was used as sort of a club.

Fewer members were now interested in going to sea on lifesaving missions so they hired lifeboat crews to do this work. But the lifesaving motifs still prevailed in the club's decorations, and there was a liturgical lifeboat in the room where initiations were held.

About this time a large ship was wrecked off the coast and the hired crews brought in loads of cold, wet, half-drowned people. They were dirty and sick and some of them had black skin and some had yellow skin.

The beautiful new club was considerably messed up. So the property committee immediately had a shower house built outside the club where the victims of shipwrecks could be cleaned up before coming inside.

At the next meeting there was a split in the club membership. Most of the members wanted to stop the club's lifesaving activities, complaining that they were unpleasant and a hindrance to the normal social life of the club.

Some members insisted upon lifesaving as their primary purpose and pointed out they were still called a lifesaving station. But they were finally voted down and told if they wanted to save the lives of various kinds of people who were shipwrecked in those waters, they could begin their own lifesaving station down the coast. They did.

As the years went by, the new station experienced the same changes that had occurred in the old. It evolved into a club, and yet another lifesaving station was founded. History continued to repeat itself, and if you visit that coast today, you will find a number of exclusive clubs along the shore. Shipwrecks are frequent in those waters, but most of the people drown.

—Author Unknown

9. Write down the name of one Christian friend whom you will disciple in the Word during the next three months.
10. Every church ought to have some type of leadership training program. This is the crux of discipleship. One such method of leadership training is the church lay institute. The lay institute provides the church with teachers, evangelistic workers, lay preachers and counselors. And it provides interested believers with the necessary training to engage in those ministries with some measure of competency.

I would like to suggest (if your church has no such program) that you consider the following format:

LEADERSHIP TRAINING INSTITUTE

a. The local church leadership training institute could provide an offering of eight lay courses on a two-year plan, developed by your own church.

b. Each course may run for twelve weeks.

c. Courses could be offered September through November, December through February, March through May, and June through August.

d. Class sessions should be no more than an hour in length and should meet in the church or a designated home on a regularly scheduled night of the week. Monday evenings are usually preferred.

e. The first four courses (offered during the first year of the cycle) should be informational and foundational, such as Bible Study Methods, Bible Survey, Bible Doctrine, and Church History.

f. The last four courses (offered during the second year of the cycle) should be practical in nature such as Evangelism, Teaching, Counseling, and Preaching.

g. As qualified teachers for the courses develop, it would be possible to offer many if not all of the courses simultaneously. This way a person could plug into the program at any time.

h. One method of gaining teachers may be to ask a prospective teacher to take the given course with the intent of teaching it next time around.

i. Upon completion of a course, the church should find placement for the trained leader if he shows sufficient spiritual maturity and continued interest. For example, if someone has taken the course in lay preaching, the church should provide him with a place of outreach ministry, such as a regular service in a nursing home, jail, hospital chapel, rescue mission, or church pulpit supply. As a matter of fact, one requirement for taking the course might well be the commitment to enter into some such type of outreach ministry. The same ought to hold true in the areas of counseling, teaching and evangelism.

j. It is good to keep the classes small and the standards high. Perhaps by limiting the classes to six or twelve at a time (depending on the size of your church) the teacher's interaction with the lay students would give more benefit to the student and more opportunity for careful evaluation on the part of the instructor.

k. Some sort of certificate could be printed by the church and presented to those completing the program. (At least five courses ought to be required of those desiring a certificate: the four basic informational courses and one practical course.) However, one should not have to obligate himself to the entire program to enjoy the benefits of any one course that may fit his interest or sense of need.

1. The following is a possible curriculum model:

First Year

	BIBLE STUDY METHODS (SEPT.-NOV.)	BIBLE SURVEY (DEC.-FEB.)	BIBLE DOCTRINE (MAR.-MAY)	CHURCH HISTORY (JUNE-AUG.)
1.	Joy of Discovery	Panorama	Introduction	Panorama
2.	Illumination	Walk Through Old Testament	Doctrine of Bible	Spread of Christianity
3.	Observation #1	Historical Books	Doctrine of God	Old Imperial Church
4.	Observation #2	Legal Books	Doctrine of Christ	Catholic Supremacy
5.	Interpretation #1	Wisdom Books	Doctrine of Holy Spirit	Medieval Christianity
6.	Interpretation #2	Prophetic Books	Doctrine of Angels	Church and State
7.	Application #1	Walk Through New Testament	Doctrine of Demons	Papal Zenith
8.	Application #2	The Gospels	Doctrine of Man	Pre-Reformation
9.	Correlation #1	Acts	Doctrine of Sin	Reformation
10.	Correlation #2	Pauline Epistles	Doctrine of Salvation	Denominationalism
11.	Using Charts	General Epistles	Doctrine of Church	Modernism
12.	Using Tools	Revelation	Doctrine of Last Things	Ecumenism and Fundamentalism
	(Note: #1 = "Laws" & #2 = "Practice")			

	EVANGELISM (SEPT.-NOV.)	TEACHING (DEC.-FEB.)	COUNSELING (MAR.-MAY)	LAY PREACHING (JUNE-AUG.)
			Second Year	
1.	The Gospel	A Philosophy of Education	Introduction & Overview	Selecting Passage
2.	The Mandate	Biblical Teaching	Secular Psychology	Studying Passage
3.	Theology of Evangelism	Teach for Results	Biblical Psychology	Stating the Idea
4.	The Principles	Laws of Teaching	Integrated Psychology	Developing Idea
5.	The Precedent	Evaluation	Conflict	Supporting Material
6.	The Plan	Curriculum	Personality Types	Transitions
7.	The Presentation	Audio Visuals	Personal Development	Illustration
8.	The Particulars	Methodology	Physical Factors	Application
9.	The Persons You May Encounter	Teaching Materials	Psychological Disorders	The Conclusion
10.	The Problems You May Face	Story Telling	Psychological Testing	The Introduction
11.	Practice	Atmosphere	Psychotherapy	Titles
12.	Preserving the Converts	Understanding Your Student	Christian Counseling	Delivery

2
Balancing
the Program

THE SWING OF THE PENDULUM

After reading the first chapter, you probably want to post the sign "Mission Impossible" in front of your church. Did you feel a little frustrated trying to get it all together in terms of incorporating both evangelism and biblical edification? That's all right. You made a noble start. The first step is *understanding* the need. Implementing the corrective process is the next step. Where do we go from here?

WHAT DID JESUS DO?

In Mark 3:14, we are told the twofold process of Christ's discipleship program: "And He appointed twelve, that they might be with Him, and that He might send them out to preach."

This verse is highly significant. Notice that after He gathered a quantity of disciples, He did two things:

(1) He spent time with them. Even a cursory reading of the Gospel accounts reveals the rigorous training program that Jesus maintained with His disciples. He instructed

31

them by discourse, object lessons, demonstration, on the job training, and dialogue. There were three ingredients in Jesus' first phase: education, edification, and equipping. Through these means, He guided His disciples into maturity. This was the "quality" aspect of His ministry with them. But how did He enlarge the number of disciples in "quantity"?

(2) He sent the disciples out to preach. Not even the omnipotent wonder-working Son of God carried the total weight of the evangelistic ministry on His own shoulders. The Scriptures tell us that for the second phase of Jesus' discipleship program, He sent the disciples out to preach!

FURTHER BIBLICAL INSTRUCTION

Later the Apostle Paul said to Pastor Timothy: "And the things which you have heard from me in the presence of many witnesses, these entrust to faithful men, who will be able to teach others also" (2 Timothy 2:2).

SIGNIFICANT OBSERVATIONS

Notice, Timothy was to follow the example of the Lord Jesus. He was to spend time entrusting the spiritual truths of the faith to his disciples, and then was to send them out to teach the faith to others! This was exactly the practice of the early New Testament local church. The assembly of the believers was not primarily intended to be an evangelistic service, for it was just what the Bible says it was—an assembly of believers! The believers were discipled with the same three ingredients as the disciples of the Lord Jesus—education, edification, and equipping, and were *then* sent out to preach!

An example of an early Christian assembly is found in

Acts 20:7. The Scriptures are careful to tell us when they met, who was present, and what was done: "And upon the first day of the week, when the disciples came together to break bread, Paul preached unto them, ready to depart on the morrow; and continued his speech until midnight" (AV).

This was not an evangelistic meeting. Paul was not preaching the gospel. The word in the original which is here translated "preached" is the word from which we get "dialogue," meaning "discussed." It is not the word for "preach" from which we get the word "evangelize." Besides, notice who was present: ". . . when the disciples came together." There was no need to preach the gospel. The believers met on the first day of the week to celebrate the Lord's Supper and receive instruction!

The Book of Acts does not stop there, however, but gives us a multitude of references to the evangelistic efforts of the equipped disciples throughout the week in the ordinary work-a-day world of the Roman Empire.

After being educated, edified, and equipped, the disciples went out from the assembly to proclaim the gospel of Christ in the marketplace, at the city gate, in the jailhouse, before politicians, in philosophical meetings, on the job, in the homes and on the streets! The early church had a balanced purpose—they were growing by leaps and bounds in both quality *and* quantity. Why? Because they implemented a balanced program after our Lord's example.

The church assembled was involved in the maturing process while the church dispersed (during the week) was involved in evangelism. This manifests a biblical balance of local church activity. Remember, the local church is not a building—it is people.

What we have discussed so far is a first-century reality

and a twentieth-century ideal! Today in our modern society it has become a respectable practice to attend church, even on the part of unregenerate individuals, in order to fulfill a felt moral obligation or ease a religiously oriented conscience.

For this reason, we will frequently have unbelievers attending our fellowship. (Interestingly, this was not unheard of even in the first century; although the assembly was primarily for believers, there were times even then when unbelievers attended, as seen for example in 1 Corinthians 14:23).

Shall we stop teaching our believers and preach a simple gospel outline Sunday after Sunday? No, we don't have to do that. The Scriptures are pregnant with the truth of redemption. It is impossible to study the Word of God and exclude any input concerning redemption. It is quite possible to build up the believers by the exposition of the whole counsel of God while at the same time making the gospel available to those who are yet without saving faith.

This is not only possible—this is our mandate. But the church should continue to be ever so careful lest the believers leave the assembly without spiritual input for themselves. The priority of the assembly must always be edification.

Evangelism must remain the priority of the "dispersion" (the individual church members in their normal contexts of life, Monday through Saturday). This evangelism may take the form of personal evangelism, a visitation program, radio broadcast, open-air meeting or literature distribution plan, but it must remain the responsibility of the members outside of the four church walls.

The letters of Paul to Timothy, a young pastor in

Ephesus, give strong evidence of the careful balance of the early church.

1. Timothy was to *equip* the believers: "And the things which you have heard from me in the presence of many witnesses, these entrust to faithful men, who will be able to teach others also" (2 Timothy 2:2).
2. Timothy was to *educate* the believers: "And the Lord's bond-servant must not be quarrelsome, but be kind to all, *able to teach,* patient when wronged, with gentleness correcting . . . "(2 Timothy 2:24, 25; emphasis added).
3. Timothy was to *edify* the believers: "Preach the word; be ready in season and out of season; reprove, rebuke, exhort, with great patience and instruction" (2 Timothy 4:2).
4. Timothy was to *evangelize* the nonbelievers: "Do the work of an evangelist" (2 Timothy 4:5c). Although Timothy was a pastor and was chiefly responsible therefore to feed the flock of God, he was not exempt from the responsibility and privilege of every believer to evangelize. This he, as well as his congregation, did.

It would be well to reflect upon Ephesians 4 in light of the program for local church activity. Paul states that spiritual gifts were given:

1. "For the equipping of the saints" (verse 12).
2. "For the work of service" (verse 12).
3. "To the building up of the body of Christ" (verse 12).
4. "Until we all attain to the unity of the faith" (verse 13). Also, the activity was to be carried out by the fellowship of mutual participation (verse

16), and in the context of worship (Ephesians 1:16).

PUTTING IT INTO PARAPHRASE

And He appointed a quantity of disciples, that they may spend time with him in training, and that they may go out and do the work of evangelism (Mark 3:14).

APPLICATION PROJECT

For the Church Leader and Layperson

1. True or false: The primary goal of our Sunday morning service is to instruct the assembled believers.
2. True or false: The gospel is made available at some time during our morning service for the sake of attending unbelievers.
3. Our church provides the following discipleship ministries:
   a. Follow-up classes for new converts
   b. "Mini-flock" get-togethers
   c. Regular "shepherding" visits
   d. Home Bible studies
   e. Leadership training
   f. Lay Institute courses
   g. None of the above
   h. All of the above
   i. Other
4. Check those areas in which your church maintains an evangelistic ministry:
   __Radio Spots
   __Radio Programming
   __Cable TV
   __Commercial TV Spots
   __Commercial TV Programming
   __Telephone
   __Newspaper
   __Mail
   __Open Air Evangelism
   __Drama
   __Films

___Literature
___Crusade
___Nursing Home
___Jail
___Rescue Mission
___Hospital
___Children's Home
___Retired Apartments
___Servicemen's Center
___Halfway House
___Day Care Center
___Release-Time Classes
___Lay Institute
___Occupational Evangelism
___Local Government
___Door-to-Door Visitation
___Prospect Visitation
___Correlated Visitation
___Home Bible Study
___Joy Club
___Neighborhood Outreach Program
___Coffee Pot Evangelism
___Church Gospel Teams
___Counseling Service
___Banquet Evangelism
___Bus Ministry
___Sunday School Evangelism
___Vacation Bible School Evangelism
___Athletics Program
___Drive-In Church
___Men's Breakfast
___Coffee House
___Tape Ministry

__International Students' Ministry
__Camp
__Fair/Rodeo Evangelism
__Coffee Stop (free coffee and gospel literature offered at a wayside rest stop during holiday travel)
__Seminars
__Wheels for Golden Agers
__Campus Evangelism

5. List 10 specific ways your church could reach out into the community evangelistically:

   1. _____
   2. _____
   3. _____
   4. _____
   5. _____
   6. _____
   7. _____
   8. _____
   9. _____
   10. _____

6. True or false: Our church recently had a training program in personal evangelism for our people.

7. What percentage of your congregation would be presently equipped to bear effective verbal witness in their everyday world:

   10%   25%   50%   75%   100%

8. Every church ought to have some form of visitation program. One good way to begin is by contacting your church's first-time visitors. If your church has no such program, lovingly suggest it to the leadership!

   Here is a simple plan that is easy to implement:

VISITATION PROGRAM

a. Personnel

    1) Secure volunteers from the congregation who are willing to make at least one visit a week at their own convenience. The total group of volunteers comprises the visitation team.

    2) Select one of the volunteers who gives evidence of leadership ability as the team leader.

    3) Secure a typist in the congregation who will commit herself to typing letters each week to first-time church visitors.

    4) Enlist the prayer support of individuals unable to assist in visitation who will nevertheless be able to support the team in specific prayer.

b. Provisions

    1) Provide all first-time visitors to the church (in all services) with a visitor's information card. These may be purchased at your local Christian bookstore.

    2) Provide the visitation secretary with an original draft of a letter you would like her to send to all the visitors. The letter should be warm, personal, informative and inviting in nature.

    3) Provide the central church office with a card catalog file to maintain visitation records.

c. Procedure

    1) Have the visitors' cards placed in the collection plates during the offering.

    2) It should then be the responsibility of the chairmen of the ushers to get the cards to the visitation secretary.

3) Once she gets the cards, the secretary types each visitor a personal letter from the pastor.
   a) Letters are signed by the pastor.
   b) Letters are sent out the following Monday.
4) Next, the secretary provides a list of the visitors for the pastor.
5) The cards are then given to the team leader.
6) The team leader distributes the cards among the visitation team members.
7) After receiving the card or cards, the team member visits the visitor's home at his convenience during the week.
8) After the visit, the number of the visit (1, 2, or 3) is marked on the upper right hand corner of the card, along with the date of visit and initials of the team member.
9) On the following Sunday, the team member files the card in the visitation file. It is filed alphabetically, and under the section corresponding to the visit number.
10) The visitor should be visited three times over a six-month period by the visitation team.
    a) Show an interest in the visitors. Get to know them personally, and invite them to return.
    b) Maintain personal interest, and inform them of the various programs of the church which may interest them.
    c) Show an interest in the visitors' spiritual welfare. Endeavor to lead them to Christ.
11) Seek them out when they return to church and make them feel genuinely welcomed.
12) Assign spiritual-sponsor families to new con-

verts for discipleship purposes.
13) Give membership prospects to membership committee.
14) Provide some kind of periodic seminar or workshop training for your visitation workers.

Here are some suggested tools:

Coleman, Robert E., *Master Plan of Evangelism, The* (Westwood: Fleming H. Revell Company, 1964)

Hirsh, Herbert L., *Winning of the Lost, The* (Published by the author: 415 N. E. 147th Terrace, Miami, FL 33161, n.d.)

Kennedy, D. James, *Evangelism Explosion* (Wheaton: Tyndale House Publishers, 1970)

Little, Paul E., *How to Give Away Your Faith* (Downers Grove: Inter-Varsity Press, 1977)

Moore, Waylon B., *New Testament Follow-Up* (Grand Rapids: Wm. B. Eerdmans Company, 1973)

Pickering, Ernest D., *Theology of Evangelism, The* (Clarks Summit, PA: Baptist Bible College Press, 1976)

3
Balancing
the People

THE SWING OF THE PENDULUM

Having looked at the purpose and the program of the local body of believers, let's direct our attention to the body of believers itself. A local assembly of Christians is a most interesting object of observation for it consists of a collection of new converts and mature saints, carnal Christians and spiritual ones, the aggressive and the reticent, the very old and the very young, the strong and the weak, the multi-talented and the uni-talented, the loud and the quiet, the creative and the traditional—all bound together under one spiritual roof.

How does such a diverse group of individuals function as a single body in the process of edifying itself in quality and quantity? Here again, there are two extremes. On the one hand, there is the strong traditional church which clearly outlines every "jot and tittle" of church practice that is to be the mold for every believer. If a person is sufficiently squeezed into the accepted church mold, he is viewed as being "spiritual." If, however, he has not completely conformed his life to meet every standard of the church, he is looked upon as "unspiritual." Such a church is often labeled as a "legalistic" church.

This type of church has discovered the biblical principle of DISCIPLINE, but has taken it to the extreme. Under such conditions, there are often many unhealthy results: (1) Spirituality becomes an external costume rather than an internal reality. (2) Conformity is practiced to "win" the love of the brethren, not because the individual has had sufficient time to grow intensely in love with the Saviour with a desire to please only Him. (3) The fruit of the Spirit no longer remains the ultimate manifestation of Christlikeness. (4) New believers are not given sufficient time to grow in grace. (5) Many carnal believers feel that they are spiritual giants because they wear the external cloaks of righteousness. (6) Christian neurotics are produced when certain believers are simply unable to completely fit the mold at their level of spiritual maturity.

There is, however, the other extreme. This is the church in which "anything goes." The norm of the church is conformity to the world, external permissiveness, and the absence of church discipline completely. This church has discovered the biblical principle of FREEDOM but has taken this principle to the extreme. There are no stable guidelines, no high standards, no controls. There is no direction or correction.

Such a church also produces many unhealthy results: (1) The Word of God becomes a doctrinal textbook instead of a vibrant precept to obey and live. (2) Spiritual maturity remains a theoretical hypothesis instead of a genuine experience. (3) Few people are in conformity to the image of Christ. (4) The Christian life is robbed of its challenge. (5) The results of spiritual health—peace, forgiveness, happiness, fruit, rewards, fellowship—are not enjoyed. (6) The example of the church presents a stumbling block instead of a testimony to the onlooking non-Christian community.

Which principle ought to be the guideline for the functioning of the local body—discipline, or freedom?

WHAT DID JESUS SAY?

Jesus said, "If you abide in My word, then you are truly disciples of Mine; and you shall know the truth, and the truth shall make you free" (John 8:31b-32).

In referring here to the Christian life, Jesus again applies the principle of balance. The true disciple, according to Jesus, has two states of being—he is one who is guided and controlled by the Word, *and* he is one who is free. The two states are to be held in perfect balance. To be sure, Jesus is here referring to freedom from the bondage of sin (verse 34). However, this is only one facet of the larger biblical doctrine of freedom of which it is a part.

Paul refers frequently to the doctrine of Christian liberty in his epistles to the Corinthians and the Galatians. He is also the most vocal of all the apostles on the subject of church discipline. What is the ingredient of spiritual living which brings discipline and freedom into a perfect balance?

FURTHER BIBLICAL INSTRUCTION

Let's look once again at Ephesians 4:16: "From whom the whole body, being fitted and held together by that which every joint supplies, according to the proper working of each individual part, causes the growth of the body for the building up of itself in love."

The underlying ingredient of the functioning Christian

body is LOVE! It is the element of LOVE which keeps the balance between church discipline and church freedom, with the end result of a healthy, growing, functioning body of believers.

Here, then, are the three principles which contribute to healthy church life—LOVE, FREEDOM, and DISCIPLINE. Love provides the expression of the individual's potential in a positive and spontaneous way needed for genuine growth. Discipline provides the controls and directives for the individual believer's spiritual welfare.

It is interesting to note that psychologist J. A. Hadfield in his book, *Childhood and Adolescence,* lists these three principles as the three cardinal principles of parenthood in the development of the child and adolescent. There is a definite and obvious parallel to the development of spiritual maturity in a local family of believers.

Hadfield states:

> These three principles, far from being incompatible, as generally supposed, are necessary to one another and to the full development of the child's personality. Only in an atmosphere of security is a child free to act, to venture, and to be spontaneous. Only by discipline can these spontaneous tendencies be directed and coordinated, so that the personality is free. Discipline, therefore, is as necessary to true freedom as freedom is necessary to true self-discipline. And a sense of security is a prerequisite to both.[1]

Let's examine these three principles and their relationship to the local church.

Love

A few years ago a song swept the country entitled, "What This World Needs Now Is Love Sweet Love." Within a Christian context, I've been waiting for someone to write the song, "What This Church Needs Now Is Love Sweet Love," referring to biblical love. A more recent hit on the top ten is entitled, "How Deep Is Your Love?" Perhaps we ought to pose this question to the local church—again referring to biblical love. But what is biblical love?

Someone has written: "Love is a funny thing, it's just like a lizard. It curls up around your heart, and jumps into your gizzard!" Still another expostulates: "Love is like an onion, we taste it with delight. But when it's gone we wonder, what ever made us bite."

Obviously, this kind of love is far too shallow to pass for biblical love. What kind of love does the Bible call for? Jesus said, "Love one another . . . as I have loved you . . ." (John 13:34). Our love for others is to be like Jesus' love for others.

The four Gospels give us a candid portrait of Jesus' love, both by means of His teaching and His example. Four characteristics of genuine love can be clearly observed.

Our love is to be a choice of the will. According to Jesus' teaching, love is not a product of feeling, but an active choice.

And whoever shall force you to go one mile, *go* with him two. *Give* to him who asks of you, and *do not turn* away from him who wants to borrow from you. You have heard that it was said, "You shall love your neighbor, and hate your enemy." But I say to you, *love* your enemies, and *pray* for those who persecute you; in order that you may be sons of your Father who is in heaven; for He causes His sun to rise on the evil and the good, and sends rain on the righteous and the unrighteous (Matthew 5:41-45; emphasis mine).

Notice the list of imperatives! Jesus does not exhort us to wait for an emotional "feeling." Here is a mark of maturity. The mature believer does not let his emotions control him. He controls his emotions. Jesus aptly and dramatically demonstrated this as He prayed on the cross, "Father, forgive them . . . " His love was most certainly not engendered by the murderous mob. His love, however, was an act of the will.

In your church, you may have an unwed mother, a backbiter, a schemer, a politician, a gossip, a young radical, a sponger, a critic. You may have someone with whom you disagree on a point of theology or a decision in the church. You may have those who do not want a choir while you do, desire a green carpet while you want red, or want to decrease the missionary budget while you want to increase it. Love them. Don't wait for an emotional lizard to jump into your gizzard. Love them. Biblical love is a choice of the will.

Our love is to be active. According to Jesus' teaching, love is the active demonstration of care and concern. As a part of His reply to the inquisitive scribe, Jesus authoritatively quotes Leviticus 19:18: " 'You shall love your neighbor as yourself' " (Mark 12:31b).

Now, I can't believe that Jesus is telling about some sensational emotional involvement. I've yet to see a mature believer embracing himself before embracing others. Obviously, He is speaking of care and concern.

We take care of ourselves. We make sure that we are clothed properly and have adequate meals. We take care of ourselves when we are sick. This is the kind of love we are to have for others.

Robert Louis Stevenson once said, "So long as we love, we serve." Jesus demonstrated this throughout His earthly ministry. The feeding of the 5,000 is merely one case in point.

Just a couple of months ago, I conducted a funeral in my church. A family lost their thirty-two year old son. Several called them to say, "I love you and am praying for you," and then there were the others—the others who didn't have to say it in words because their actions said it for them. One family stayed around the clock with the bereaved family at the hospital. A second family provided all the meals. Another family provided transportation. This is biblical love.

W. Stanley Mooneyham made an interesting statement in *Christianity Today,* "Love talked about is easily turned aside, but love demonstrated is irresistible."[2]

In his classic work, *The Art of Loving,* Erich Fromm writes:

Love is an activity, not a passive affect [sic]; it is a "standing in," not a "falling for." In the most general way, the active character of love can be described by stating that love is primarily *giving,* not receiving.[3]

So, then, our love is not only to be a choice of the will; it is to be active as well. But there are still two more characteristics.

Our love is to be unconditional. According to Jesus' teaching, love is not based upon the "worth" of the recipient. Luke complements Matthew's account of Christ's Sermon on the Mount by recording these words:

> And if you love those who love you, what credit is that to you? For even sinners love those who love them. And if you do good to those who do good to you, what credit is that to you? For even sinners do the same thing. And if you lend to those from whom you expect to receive, what credit is that to you? Even sinners lend to sinners, in order to receive back the same amount. But love your enemies, and do good, and lend, expecting nothing in return; and your reward will be great, and you will be sons of the Most High; for He Himself is kind to ungrateful and evil men (Luke 6:32-35).

It is vitally important to recognize the existence of two types of love—*intrinsic* and *extrinsic*. Simply stated, *intrinsic love* is acceptance of, care and affection for an individual *regardless of and in spite of* that individual's performance, strengths, weaknesses, or reciprocal feeling.

This is the kind of love which God has for each of us. "But God demonstrates His own love toward us, in that while we were yet sinners, Christ died for us"(Romans 5:8). God loves those who don't even love Him first. He loves the unlovely. He loves the weak. He loves the fallen. He loves those who are His enemies. He loves you and me.

Of all the truths of the Christian gospel, the one with which I am comforted the most is the truth that I will always stand in God's love because His love for me is unconditional. "For I am convinced that neither death, nor life, nor angels, nor principalities, nor things present, nor things to come, nor powers, nor height, nor depth, nor any other created thing, shall be able to separate us from the love of God, which is in Christ Jesus our Lord" (Romans 8:38-39). This is intrinsic—unconditional love.

Even Shakespeare acknowledged, "We must love men ere they seem worthy of our love." Perhaps the most striking example to me was the unconditional love of one woman who lost her missionary husband to the murderous Auca Indians in South America. On one occasion I saw her introduce a beloved brother in Christ to a student chapel audience. It was the man who had killed her husband prior to his conversion.

We have many opportunities to love unconditionally in the local church; to love the long-haired radical who attends our fellowship, to love the deacon who always votes against us; to love the parishioner who refuses to shake hands. Such love is supernatural. But I warn you, such love is contagious.

In contrast, *extrinsic love* is acceptance of and care and affection for an individual *due* to that individual's performance, strengths, and reciprocal feeling. This is the kind of love that says, "If you love me, then I will love you back." It is the kind of love that says, "If you live up to my ideals, live the way I do, dress the way I do, talk the way I do and think the way I do, then I will love you."

Let's be honest. Which of these two types of love do you feel more accurately portrays the love which we usually experience in the local church? Do you want to hear some explosive words from the lips of our Saviour? Listen to this, "A new commandment I give to you, that you love one another, *even as I have loved you,* that you also love one another" (John 13:34; emphasis mine).

Intrinsic unconditional love is the underlying principle of the Christian life, and it is the underlying principle of local church fellowship. With this type of secure love, discipline will be received graciously and freedom will not be exploited.

In the inspirational classic, *The Greatest Thing in the World,* Henry Drummond writes:

> Love is patient. This is the normal attitude of love . . . love waiting to begin; not in a hurry; calm; ready to do its work when the summons comes but meantime wearing the ornament of a meek and quiet spirit. Love suffers long; beareth all things; believeth all things; hopeth all things. For love understands, and therefore waits.[4]

Intrinsic, patient love is no respecter of persons. In a local church, this kind of love accepts the strong and the weak; the victorious and the fallen; the mature and the babes in Christ. "For love understands, and therefore waits."[5] Yet there remains one more characteristic.

Our love is to be sacrificial. According to Jesus' teaching, love knows no sacrifice that is too great. He said, "Greater love has no one than this, that one lay down his life for his friends. You are My friends, if you do what I command you" (John 15:13-14). Jesus Himself also demonstrated these words in the highest possible sense when He died for the sins of the world, effecting a substitutionary atonement. Love costs.

One does not always have the opportunity to demonstrate love by ultimate sacrifice. Yet there are examples. The Associated Press released one article about a Polish POW named Maksymilian Kolbe who died in the place of Franciszek Gajowniczek, a fellow POW.

Does Christ expect us all to die for a friend? Of course not. What He does expect, however, is a love willing to make sacrifices. Frederick Agar once said, "Love never asks how much *must* I do, but how much *can* I do."

One does not have to have the gift of helps to express his love to fellow believers in the local assembly. Are you willing to sacrifice an hour of your time to visit with an elderly widow or prepare a tasty meal for a shut-in? Are you willing to pick up the Jones' children for Sunday School? Are you willing to sacrifice your brilliant idea for the sake of harmony in the church? Love is sacrificial.

This, then, is the kind of love which flourishes in the healthy local church. It is a choice of the will. It is active. It is unconditional. It is sacrificial.

Freedom

During my last year at college I enrolled in a course taught by a professor who had befriended me and won my strong admiration. In contrast to my stuttering speech, disorganization and lack of social graces, he possessed the clearest enunciation, the utmost of organization, and a mastery of social graces. After a few days I became very threatened in his class and around him as my professor.

I felt, at times, that his image of me was much too high. As a result, I felt tremendously pressured to produce a higher quality of work than I was capable of doing so as not to disappoint him since his standard of excellence was so very high. At other times, I felt that his image of me must be terribly low. As a result, I felt greatly pressured to produce a higher quality of work than I was capable of doing, so as to make a better impression upon him. Finally, I became too discouraged to even attempt my homework.

At last, I decided to go to his office and let him know exactly what I was thinking. After relating my dilemma to him, I said, "Prof, what I have come to ask you for is the freedom to fail or succeed and the freedom to be myself, knowing that after this course is over you will still respect me as your friend regardless of my work."

With moist eyes and a smile, he responded, "Gary, that freedom is yours. Regardless of your performance in my class, I will always respect you as a student and a friend." I cannot express the intense motivation that I then received in the work that lay before me. That professor's intrinsic love for me as a student provided the freedom that I needed in which to excel.

That is the kind of freedom which I feel is so urgently needed in the local church. Young Christians need the freedom to be themselves. They need the freedom to grow in grace spontaneously. They need the freedom to be transparent. They need the freedom to fail as well as succeed. They need the freedom to reveal their weaknesses as well as their strengths. They need the freedom to be creative and different so that their love for Jesus Christ will be their very own love and not a carbon copy of someone else's.

Too often a church member is afraid to let his fellow brethren know of his weaknesses or spiritual failures, and struggles for fear that he will be looked upon less favorably, perhaps as a carnal Christian, and therefore, sad but true, unaccepted by the congregation (many of which are also struggling with the same weaknesses)! This is why the average church member chooses to wear a facade—a pseudo-spiritual image—always wearing a smile, praising the Lord, shouting "Amen," and vocally condemning other Christians who are not as "spiritual." All this is being done while on the inside the individual might himself be weak, defeated and trying with all his might to break a sinful habit.

If only the local body would admit that every believer is in the same category—no one is living in the glorified state yet! All of us have strengths and weaknesses. All of us have spiritual struggles. All of us experience times of defeat.

The great need in today's local church is the freedom to be honest and open with the Lord, ourselves, and others without the threat of rejection lurking over our heads! What potential spiritual growth would belong to that local assembly where the members were free to ask for prayer during a spiritual crisis while at the same time knowing that those who were praying for them today might be the very ones in need of their prayers tomorrow.

Freedom is essential to genuine spiritual growth. Spiritual growth is spontaneous—it is not the product of coercion. Coercion might produce conformable automatons but it will never produce genuine spirituality. The old Baptists who fought so vigorously for religious freedom realized that a church cannot legislate spirituality. Spirituality comes from within—not from without.

Well did Martin Luther say:

> But that a pope or a bishop anoints, confers, tonsures, ordains, consecrates, or prescribes dress unlike that of the laity—this may make hypocrites and graven images, but it never makes a Christian or "spiritual" man.[6]

Just as externals do not make the pastor a spiritual man, they do not make the church member a spiritual man either. Galatians 5:22-23 states: "But the fruit of the Spirit is love, joy, peace, patience, kindness, goodness, faithfulness, gentleness, self-control; against such things there is no law."

We must not demand a one-year-old in the Lord to walk like a five-year-old in the Lord. We must lovingly share the Word of God in prayer and patience, and give the young believer the freedom and guidance he needs to mature in the Lord spontaneously and willingly, bearing the fruit of the Spirit. Perhaps this will spare many from becoming neurotic Christians or spiritual automatons.[7]

Freedom, however, does not mean license. We must not forget the point of our discussion. Balance is the key word. Let's quote again those words from Hadfield:

> Only by discipline can these spontaneous tendencies be directed and coordinated, so that the personality is free. Discipline, therefore, is as necessary to true freedom as freedom is necessary to true self-discipline.[8]

Freedom without discipline is unwise, unhealthy, and unscriptural. In a very true sense, freedom without discipline is *not* freedom among a closely knit group of individuals such as you have in a local church; for with freedom comes responsibility—and that responsibility is grounded on God's Word.

Discipline

In his book, *The Church at the End of the 20th Century,* Francis Schaeffer very wisely states:

> So often people think that Christianity is only something soft, only a kind of gooey love that loves evil equally with good. This is not the biblical position. The holiness of God is to be exhibited simultaneously with love. We must be careful, therefore, not to say that what is wrong is right,

whether it is in the area of doctrine or of life, in our own group or another. Anywhere what is wrong is wrong, and we have a responsibility in that situation to say that what is wrong is wrong. But the observable love must be there regardless of the cost.[9]

Although intrinsic love always accepts a person, the Christian by means of mutual supportive edification, seeks to encourage another unto godliness, and does all he can to flee from sin and encourage his fellow believers to do the same. This principle is called *discipline.*

There are two kinds of discipline, both of which are scriptural and both of which are to be practiced by the local assembly—*preventive* and *corrective.* Preventive church discipline consists of direction, guidance, and warning. The Scriptures are full of directives, guidelines, and warnings. Even under grace, obedience is never optional. God gave these preventatives because He loves us and wants the very best for us. These are given to keep the Christian from falling into those sins which bring contempt upon the body of Christ and therefore, Christ Himself.

There are times, though, when even the most well-meaning Christian falls into such sin. Concerning such a Christian the Bible says:

"My son, do not regard lightly the discipline of the Lord, nor faint when you are reproved by Him; for those whom the Lord loves He disciplines, and He scourges every son whom He receives." It is for discipline that you endure; God deals with you as with sons; for what son is there whom his father does not discipline? (Hebrews 12:5b-7).

IS MY CHURCH WHAT GOD MEANT IT TO BE?

It is no secret in the New Testament that God disciplines His children. In this regard, He has given several guidelines to the local church concerning the implementation of discipline. These guidelines involve three kinds of sin—personal, private, and public. Since it is not the purpose of this discussion to present a systematic church administration plan, I will only touch briefly on these guidelines.

First, we are told in the Scriptures that a Christian is to deal with personal sins *personally.* That is, when a Christian has fallen into some area of sin that is known only to him, the issue is to be dealt with between that individual and God. First John 1:9 states, "If we confess our sins, He is faithful and righteous to forgive us our sins and to cleanse us from all unrighteousness."

It is the work of the Spirit of God that brings a believer to a place of confession and restoration in such instances. However, if the believer finds himself ensnared in a habit which he cannot seem to break, he is encouraged to share his dilemma with a fellow believer or fellow believers who will be able to give him wise loving counsel and prayer support to the end that he will experience victory. James 5:16 states, "Therefore, confess your sins to one another, and pray for one another, so that you may be healed. The effective prayer of a righteous man can accomplish much."

Secondly, we are told in the Scriptures that a Christian is to deal with private sins *privately.* Here I am referring to an incident between two Christian brothers, or a small group of believers within the church. This guideline is laid down for us in Matthew 18:15-16:

> And if your brother sins, go and reprove him in private; if he listens to you, you have won your

brother. But if he does not listen to you, take one or two more with you, so that by the mouth of two or three witnesses every fact may be confirmed.

In other words, the principle behind this guideline is this: *The offended one goes to the offender.* This is the principle that Jesus Christ Himself established for us.

Finally, there are those times when a believer will fall into a sin which will be known *publicly* to the other believers of the assembly, and even to individuals outside of the church. Such an incident does bring reproach upon the church and upon Christ Himself. Such sins include the disregard of authority (Matthew 18:17; 1 Thessalonians 5:14); contention (Romans 16:17; 1 Corinthians 11:16; Titus 3:9, 10); false doctrine (Galatians 1:9; 1 Timothy 1:19, 20; 6:1-5); going to law against a fellow believer (1 Corinthians 6:5-7); and immorality (1 Corinthians 5:11; Ephesians 5:5).

Once again, just as personal sin is to be dealt with personally and private sin privately, public sin is to be dealt with publicly. It should be remembered, here, however, that discipline toward a believer is to be *corrective*—not *punitive*—for the goal of church discipline is restoration.

This is clearly seen in Paul's Corinthian epistles. Not only did Paul exhort the Corinthian church to discipline publicly the brother who was guilty of gross immorality, but after the repentance of the brother, Paul charged the church: ". . . You should rather forgive and comfort him, lest somehow such a one be overwhelmed by excessive sorrow. Wherefore I urge you to reaffirm your love for him" (2 Corinthians 2:7-8). It is extremely interesting that churches which are slow to discipline are usually also slow to forgive and restore.

You might say, "This is all very fine theoretically, but

will it work today in the twentieth-century church?'' The answer is yes. The following is a genuine example of loving biblical discipline. A young member of a northeastern fundamental Baptist church became pregnant out of wedlock. After the problem was dealt with and the penitent girl was lovingly counseled, the church made this public announcement:

> Because of the sins of fornication and illegitimate conception _____ was placed under church discipline by the Board of Elders of the _____ Church. _____ admitted her sin of violation of the law of God, revealed a genuinely repentant attitude and expressed the desire that her case be used as a deterring force among our young people. Therefore, the Board of Elders unanimously advises that _____ retain the privileges of church membership and requests that the church watch over her in kindness, brotherly love, and in prayer. Furthermore, the Board of Elders urges the church make every effort to hold a standard of holy living before the world continually.

Oddly enough, there are some in the evangelical camp who feel that the more severe their discipline is and the longer they wait to forgive and forget, the more spiritual they are. Actually, nothing could be further from the truth. The Bible says in Galatians 6:1-2:

> Brethren, even if a man is caught in any trespass, you who are spiritual, restore such a one in a spirit of gentleness; looking to yourself, lest you too be tempted. Bear one another's burdens, and thus fulfill the law of Christ.

Discipline *must not be avoided,* however, for it is the tool of God to keep the church pure, restrain others from sin, and restore the erring brother to sweet fellowship with the Lord and his understanding fellow believers. Love, freedom, and discipline must go hand in hand for a healthy functioning local Christian body.

In summary of our discussion thus far, it can be stated that dominance, over-coercion, perfectionism, and over-protection produce fear, anxiety, guilt, facades, mere external conformity, and spiritual self-consciousness (what do others think about me?). A healthy church is not, therefore, characterized by *over-control.*

On the other hand, neglect and nonconcern produce permissiveness, spiritual apathy, and scriptural violations. A healthy church is therefore not characterized by *under-control.* A balance of love, freedom, and discipline produces a healthy church body, which is self-acceptant, prone to self-discipline, and in the process of maturity in relationship to genuine spiritual growth and vibrant reproduction.

There remain two additional principles which need to be brought into focus in attempting to reach a balanced functioning of the local church—the principle of *fellowship,* and the principle of *spiritual service.* These two principles involve the experiential side of love, freedom, and discipline.

Fellowship

In spite of general public opinion, fellowship does not mean sharing coffee and donuts. It means much more. The word "fellowship" comes from a Greek word *koinonia,* meaning "mutual participation." According to Ephesians 4:16, Christian fellowship involves mutual participation in the process of edifying the body of Christ in love.

As we discussed in the two previous chapters, this edification is both qualitative and quantitative. Concerning qualitative mutual edification, Ray Stedman writes:

> What is terribly missing is the experience of "body life:" that warm fellowship of Christian with Christian which the New Testament calls koinonia, and which was an essential part of early Christianity. The New Testament lays heavy emphasis upon the need for Christians to know each other, closely and intimately enough to be able to bear one another's burdens, confess faults one to another, minister to one another with the word and through song and prayer, and thus come to comprehend *with all saints* as Paul puts it, *what is the breadth and length and height and depth, and to know the love of Christ which surpasses knowledge* (Ephesians 3:18,19).[10]

It can be said, then, that genuine Christian fellowship presupposes mutual goals. The mutual goals involve qualitative and quantitative edification. By quantitative edification, I mean what Paul referred to as the fellowship of the gospel—the joining of hands in biblical evangelism. By qualitative edification, I mean the process of spiritual maturity. Not only does genuine fellowship presuppose mutual goals, but it also presupposes transparency. It demands the setting aside of all facades and images. Fellowship can only exist where people allow themselves to be themselves—to be open and honest with each other and the Lord.

Stedman continues:

Another direct exhortation from the Word is that of James 5:16: *"Confess your sins one to another, and pray for one another that you may be healed."* Confessing faults certainly means to admit weaknesses and to acknowledge failures in living as Christians. It is often difficult to get Christians to do this, despite the clear directive of the Word. It goes against the grain to give an image of oneself that is anything less than perfect, and many Christians imagine that they will be rejected by others if they admit to any faults. But nothing could be more destructive to Christian koinonia than the common practice today of pretending not to have any problems. It is often true that Christian homes may be filled with bickering, squabbling, angry tantrums, even bodily attacks of one member of the family against another, and yet not one word of this is breathed to anyone else and the impression is carefully cultivated before other Christians that this is an ideal Christian family with no problems of any serious consequence to be worked out.[11]

This kind of genuineness would not only be an explosive force in the lives of Christian families, onlooking youth and new converts, but it would undoubtedly give to the seeking unbeliever a promise of reality. However, I'm not so sure this process has to take place during a prescribed regular meeting of the church.

I have attended "body life services" which proved to be awfully embarrassing. In one of them some things were confessed that should never have been revealed in a public meeting. In still another, I heard nothing but an hour of petty rambling. Although I warmly appreciate the important principles of the "body life movement," I personally do not believe that the early church made a protracted decision to have "koinonia" from 6:00-8:30 on Sunday evenings. Rather, it was a continual attitude of relationship and interdependence among the believers throughout the week. This was where the genuineness and spontaneity of the koinonia revealed itself.

According to Acts 2:42, the members of the local church in Jerusalem "were continually devoting themselves to . . . fellowship." There was a sense of church community. The need of one became the need of all.

I have had close association with a church that never conducted a protracted "body life meeting" but experienced an enormous deal of "body life" among its members during the week. Meals were shared in homes. A group of mechanically inclined members got together to fix the car of a less mechanically inclined brother. A group of housewives in the church regularly visited an elderly widow. Exhortation took place in the coffee shop. Prayer times were shared at the public school by teen believers from the local assembly. There was a feeling of mutual acceptance and joint participation in the matters of spiritual growth and evangelism, both in and out of "church" responsibilities.

This does not exclude the validity of "body life meetings"—as long as they are not substituted for church community, and as long as they are conducted tastefully and with adequate controls. The public meeting is not always the place for total transparency or self-disclosure. Proverbs 29:11a warns us, "A fool uttereth all his mind" (AV).

One lady recently heard a preacher admit that he had continual battles with sexual lust. Needless to say, this lady is still recovering from the shock. While his honesty is commendable, I must question his taste in being this candid. Perhaps there is an insecure, weak young woman in the congregation who would seek to take advantage of her pastor's confessed weakness. Or, worse yet, this pastor's perfectly normal expressions of friendship in the future could be misinterpreted by anyone who heard his confession.

The point of fellowship, however, is that genuineness is presupposed. Both hypocrisy and blatant self-disclosure are out of the question. The above preacher could have admitted his human frailty without giving the specifics to the congregation.

But how does this attitude really manifest itself in the congregation? It means that the congregation, including the leadership, will be marked by sensitivity, teachability, and flexibility. It means that everyone will recognize his own depravity and not demand perfection from the others. It means that every member will be at least willing to submit to the wishes of others without having his own way. It means that healthy, constructive criticism will be well received by all and unhealthy criticism will be forsaken.

For this fellowship does not only presuppose mutual goals and genuineness, but it also presupposes the balanced blend of love, freedom, and discipline. Again quoting from Schaeffer's appendix:

> What, then, does this love mean? How can it be made visible?
>
> First, it means a very simple thing: It means that when I have made a mistake and when I have failed to love my Christian brother, I go to him and say, "I'm sorry." That is first. . . .

How well have we consciously practiced this? How often in the power of the Holy Spirit have we gone to Christians in our own group and said, "I'm sorry"? How frequently has one group gone to another group with whom it differed and has said, "We're sorry"? It is so important that it is, for all practical purposes, a part of the preaching of the gospel itself. The observable practice of truth and the observable practice of love go hand in hand with the proclamation of the good news of Jesus Christ.[12]

Fellowship can thus be defined as a mutual participation with other believers to strive for the mutual goal of quantitative and qualitative edification, within the spiritual atmosphere of openness, love, freedom, and discipline.

Now that we have established what fellowship is, exactly what does each believer do in this joint effort of edification? This question leads us to the principle of *spiritual service.*

Spiritual Service

With the contemporary outbreak of interest in spiritual gifts, a new set of extremes has again developed. Some new churches, freshly enamored with the spiritual gift concept, see the pastor-teacher office as unnecessary, and therefore play down the importance of a full-time "preacher" in their congregation. It is their opinion that the individual members, each equipped with one or more spiritual gifts, are sufficient in themselves for the growth of the church.

On the opposite side of the spectrum, a great multitude of pastors and congregations feel that it is the job of the pastor and church officers alone to minister to the congregation, while the other members simply sit and listen. Once again, the biblical view is one of balance. We will deal with the work of the minister proper in some following chapters. For now, let's consider the spiritual ministry of the congregation. Again, Ray Stedman writes:

> The church is primarily and fundamentally a body designed to express through each individual member the life of an indwelling Lord and is equipped by the Holy Spirit with gifts designed to express that life. It follows that there could hardly be anything more abortive or pathetic than a church which fails to understand this and substitutes instead the business methods, organizational proceedings and pressure politics of the world to accomplish this work. That is a certain recipe for frustration and ultimate death. But to rediscover the divine program for the operation of a church is exciting and challenging.[13]

This view is emphatically echoed by Larry Richards: "The concept is this: *the ministry is to be mutual.* The ministry is the function of the whole people of God."[14] Richards continues to say that this ministry is implemented by the utilization of spiritual gifts.

The New Hampshire Baptist Confession of 1891 stated:

> We believe the scriptures teach that a visible Church of Christ is a congregation of baptized believers, associated by covenant in the faith and fellowship of the Gospel; observing the ordinances of Christ; governed by His laws; and exercising the gifts . . .[15]

IS MY CHURCH WHAT GOD MEANT IT TO BE?

What exactly does the Bible say about spiritual gifts? In order to get to the heart of the matter, we will go to the Scriptures with these eight questions: (a) To whom are spiritual gifts given? (b) By whom are spiritual gifts given? (c) Why are spiritual gifts given? (d) What are the spiritual gifts? (e) What gifts are given today? (f) How can I discover my spiritual gifts? (g) What should I do? (h) What should I not do?

(a) *To whom are spiritual gifts given?* The Bible makes it perfectly clear that *every* regenerated child of God is given at least one spiritual gift. "Now there are varieties of gifts, but the same Spirit. And there are varieties of ministries, and the same Lord. And there are varieties of effects, but the same God who works all things in all persons. But to each one is given the manifestation of the Spirit for the common good" (1 Corinthians 12:4-7).

Most Bible students believe that these spiritual gifts are given the moment the Holy Spirit begins to indwell the believer, which is an event contemporaneous with conversion.

(b) *By whom are spiritual gifts given?* The Bible again makes it clear that the One bestowing these special spiritual abilities is none other than the third person of the Godhead—the Holy Spirit. "But one and the same Spirit works all these things, distributing to each one individually just as He wills" (1 Corinthians 12:11).

It should be mentioned here that a spiritual gift should not be confused with a natural talent. While it is true that God is the giver of every wholesome talent, spiritual gifts are special abilities sovereignly bestowed upon a believer upon conversion for a unique *spiritual* ministry.

The original text also makes it clear that these are "grace gifts." In other words, a Christian is not given a spiritual gift because he has earned it or deserves it. As a matter of fact, quite the contrary is true. As condemned violators of the laws of God, sinners are saved totally despite their spiritual weakness and failure, because of His grace in providing the perfect substitute for our punishment—Jesus Christ, His Son.

The same is true with spiritual gifts. Not only are we undeserving of the privilege of being in God's service; we have *no right* to be involved or receive any special ability by which to serve Him. It is completely due to God's grace that He willingly and lovingly gives to us these spiritual gifts. There exists no reason in the world why a believer should look proudly upon his special ability.

(c) *Why are spiritual gifts given?* In referring to gifts of spiritual leadership, Paul teaches in Ephesians 4:12-13 that they are given:

> . . . for the equipping of the saints for the work of service, to the building up of the body of Christ; until we all attain to the unity of the faith, and of the knowledge of the Son of God, to a mature man, to the measure of the stature which belongs to the fulness of Christ.

This is significant. Those who have gifts of spiritual leadership are to equip the other members of the local body, who also have been given different spiritual gifts, for the "work of service" which he defines as the "building up of the body of Christ"! It is made clear that *all* spiritual gifts are given to build up the body of Christ, again, both in QUANTITY and QUALITY to the glory of God! Here is the four-fold responsibility of equipping, edification, education and evangelism. The local body will only be healthy in its functioning if every believer contributes the use of his or her special divine ability in the process of mutual discipleship.

> For just as we have many members in one body and all the members do not have the same function, so we, who are many, are one body in Christ, and individually members one of another. And since we have gifts that differ according to the grace given to us, let each exercise them accordingly (Romans 12:4-6a).

Again, Paul writes:

> But now God has placed the members, each one of them, in the body, just as He desired. And if they were all one member, where would the body be? But now there are many members, but one body. And the eye cannot say to the hand, "I have no need of you"; or again the head to the feet, "I have no need of you." On the contrary, it is much truer that the members of the body which seem to be weaker are necessary; and those members of the body, which we deem less honorable, on these we bestow more abundant honor, and our unseemly members come to have more abundant seemliness (1 Corinthians 12:18-23).

I appreciate the way Richards words it:

> What we see then when we look at the teaching on spiritual gifts is the church, as people, involved in one another's lives—involved in sharing with others what they themselves have received from Christ. It is the members of Christ's body being with each other and in their shared love and shared life discovering that the Spirit within each flows out. That the Spirit

within taps the special ability He has given each to contribute, and so nurtures the life of God and forms the character of God in each believing individual.

This is the church. And this is the way God planned the ministry. Each of us is needed, and each has ability to contribute.[16]

(d) *What are the spiritual gifts?* There are five lists of spiritual gifts given in the Bible. They are found in 1 Corinthians 12:8-10, 28; Romans 12:6-8; Ephesians 4:11; and 1 Peter 4:11. The lists are not identical, nor are they completely different. Together they refer to eighteen different gifts (see chart).

(e) *What gifts are given for today?* With the exception of those special phenomenal abilities given to reveal and authenticate God's Word before the Bible was completed,[17] we find nine spiritual gifts listed which you and I might possess. Just what are these spiritual gifts?

The spiritual gift of *faith* is that God-given ability to trust Him for big things, and to pray consistently with an unusual amount of confidence.

Teaching is the capability of making clear the rich truths of the Word of God with accuracy and simplicity.

Those who have the spiritual gift of *service* have an unusual capacity for helping others. This might take the form of hospitality in the home, benevolence in someone else's home, or the enduring ability to work happily behind the scenes to the glory of God.

The gift of *exhortation* can take the shape of public speaking or one-to-one counseling, but always has one unique function—the edification of believers. This may include encouragement, comfort, warning or rebuke.

IS MY CHURCH WHAT GOD MEANT IT TO BE?

	1 CORINTHIANS 12:8-10	1 CORINTHIANS 12:28	ROMANS 12:6-8	EPHESIANS 4:11	1 PETER 4:11
1.	Word of wisdom				
2.	Word of knowledge				
3.	Faith				
4.	Healing	Healings			
5.	Miracles	Miracles			
6.	Prophecy	Prophets	Prophecy	Prophets	
7.	Distinguishing of spirits				
8.	Tongues	Tongues			
9.	Interpretation of tongues				
10.		Apostles		Apostles	
11.		Teachers	Teachers	Teachers	
12.		Helps	Serving		
13.		Administration	Leading		
14.			Exhortation		
15.			Giving		
16.			Mercy		
17.				Evangelists	Serving
18.				Pastors	Speaking

74

Giving is also a spiritual gift. It is the special ability to give and to give and to give. Financial giving of significant proportion and regularity is primarily in view, but giving goes way beyond. It includes a giving attitude and ability with everything, and in every possible way.

Compassion and grace characterize the believer who possesses the gift of *mercy*. He has the sweet ability to empathize. He has a special care for those who have fallen, those who are going through trials, or those who suffer rejection.

Evangelism is the ability to lead people to Jesus Christ with unusual effectiveness. This may take the form of personal evangelism or mass evangelism.

Finally, the gift of *pastoring* is the divinely given knack for shepherding the people of God. Feeding, guiding and protecting are all a part of this shepherding care.

(f) *How can I discover my spiritual gifts?* Many Bible teachers suggest four steps for the individual believer to take:

1) It is the norm that when God bestows a spiritual gift to a believer, He also gives that believer a *desire* to be actively engaged in that particular facet of service. In other words, if God has given you the gift of teaching, you will have the desire to teach. If He has given you the gift of helps, you will have the desire to offer an unusual amount of help to your fellow believers.

2) Learning comes by doing. In order to know where you are especially gifted in the "ministry," you must get actively involved in the "ministry." Experience is usually a good teacher.

3) Other believers will recognize your gift. If no one else in the world agrees that you have the gift of teaching, it is probably safe to assume that that just isn't your gift. In the New Testament era, a believer's spiritual gift was

recognized by his fellow comrades.

4) You will experience some measure of success in that given area of ministry. If you believe that you have the gift of exhortation and your fellow Christians leave your counsel more defeated and depressed than when they came to you, you should seriously reconsider whether that is your spiritual gift.

(g) *What should I do?* Begin now to look for opportunities for service in your local church. It may not be an official position. In all likelihood, it will not be. Make it a point to encourage your discouraged brethren at every opportunity, if you think your gift might be exhortation. If you think your gift might be the gift of helps, you will not need to look very far for an opportunity to serve. If you think your gift is teaching, let the pastors know of your interest. The point is this: The first step is to get busy in the "work of service" unto the edification of the body of Christ!

(h) *What should I NOT do?* The doctrine of spiritual gifts can be very dangerous if it is abused. Here are four points of caution:

1) Do not substitute a spiritual gift in the place of LOVE for the brethren. 1 Corinthians 13:1-3 boldly declares:

> If I speak with the tongues of men and of angels, but do not have love, I have become a noisy gong or a clanging cymbal. And if I have the gift of prophecy, and know all mysteries and all knowledge; and if I have all faith, so as to remove mountains, but do not have love, I am nothing. And if I give all my possessions to feed the poor, and if I deliver my body to be burned, but do not have love, it profits me nothing.

2) Do not neglect other responsibilities by hiding behind your spiritual gift! How often I have heard someone say, "Oh, no. I don't witness. Evangelism just isn't my spiritual gift!" While it is true that God hasn't given a special unusual ability in evangelism to every Christian, *every Christian* is responsible to evangelize! Paul even told Timothy, who had the gift of pastor-teacher to "do the work of an evangelist" (2 Timothy 4:5).

In the same way, Christians who do not possess the gift of giving are responsible to uphold the work of God financially, and Christians who do not have the gift of helps are nevertheless responsible to "do good unto all men." We must not hide behind our spiritual gifts. We are to excel in the area of our gift, but we are not free of responsibility in the other areas of service.

3) Do not take pride in your spiritual gift. Remember, a spiritual gift is given by the grace of God and for the ultimate purpose of bringing glory to Him! Peter well states:

> As each one has received a special gift, employ it in serving one another, as good stewards of the manifold grace of God. Whoever speaks, let him speak, as it were, the utterances of God; whoever serves, let him do so as by the strength which God supplies; so that in all things God may be glorified through Jesus Christ, to whom belongs the glory and dominion forever and ever. Amen (1 Peter 4:10-11).

4) Do not limit your ministry to your spiritual gift. Some very necessary words of caution and significant observations have been expressed by Gene A. Getz, founder of the Fellowship Bible Church in Dallas, Texas,

and an adjunct professor at Dallas Theological Seminary. By way of warning, Dr. Getz explains:

There is an unfortunate bewilderment among evangelicals regarding spiritual gifts. I've seen some of the men I work with struggle with this problem. Some have been given the idea that they must discover their spiritual gifts before they can begin serving Jesus Christ. Unfortunately, this is putting the cart before the horse. The Bible teaches that we must begin by *becoming a man of God.* We must begin where Paul began. If one desires to be a spiritual leader in the church, it's a "fine work" he desires to do. But we must make sure we have developed the qualities that are specified in 1 Timothy 3 and Titus 1.[18]

Concerning these spiritual qualifications, Getz makes this important observation:

Paul did not say look for men with the gift of pastor-teacher, or the gift of administration, or the gift of helps, or the gift of exhortation. In fact, there is very little reference to an ability or a skill. Rather, out of the twenty qualifications listed, nineteen have to do with a man's reputation, ethics, morality, temperament, habits, and spiritual and psychological maturity. And the other one has to do with his ability to lead his own family.[19]

This reminder helps us to keep the matter of spiritual gifts in the proper perspective. All too often, churches have become so preoccupied with spiritual gifts that the body function of the believers has become greatly imbalanced. Although the Bible contains some significant information concerning spiritual gifts, which we have just surveyed, it maintains a perfect balance between spiritual gifts and spiritual qualities, the latter of which are all too frequently ignored.

Getz also makes some significant observations concerning the nature and use of spiritual gifts which the church must solemnly consider lest it be carried off into spiritual gift extremism. Perhaps the most significant is that the New Testament church with the greatest manifestation of certain spiritual gifts was also the most carnal.[20] Based upon this and other observations which he enumerates, Getz draws these three conclusions which are worthy of our careful consideration:

> *First, it is very clear that spiritual maturity and the possession and manifestation of spiritual gifts are not synonymous;* nor does individual maturity depend upon the presence of spiritual gifts. Paul evaluated maturity in the body by the degree of love, faith, and hope that was being manifested (1 Corinthians 13:13).

> *Second, since there is no uniform list of spiritual gifts given in the New Testament, obviously the writers of the New Testament were not concerned about absolute consistency in describing spiritual gifts.* Furthermore, the sum total of gifts listed in the New Testament was not manifested in every church.

> *Third, God obviously did not want to lock us into a "list of gifts."* He has not established absolute patterns in this area—which is clear from the variation that was present—even in the New Testament churches. He perhaps has left the "gift list" openended because He desires to manifest certain gifts at

various times and at various places.[21]

What, then, is the purpose of our lengthy discussion of spiritual gifts? How can we practically come to a balanced perspective of the biblical teaching of body function? Both spiritual qualities and spiritual abilities are received vertically—that is, from above. They are both manifested horizontally, with the result of the edification of the body of Christ, which, in turn, brings glory to God. Both of them, therefore, are a means to an end. When either of them becomes an end in itself, it has crossed beyond the border of biblical balance.

Kept in their proper place, however, both spiritual qualities and spiritual abilities become the means for the necessary mutual expression which we call body function. "The important issue . . . is quite clear as you study body function," Getz continues. "Christians cannot grow effectively in isolation! They need to experience each other."[22]

In conclusion, then, we can say that these five major principles—LOVE, FREEDOM, DISCIPLINE, FELLOWSHIP, and SPIRITUAL SERVICE—must be kept in balance if the local body of believers is to function healthily in the process of quantitative and qualitative edification to the glory of God.

PUTTING IT INTO PARAPHRASE

If you live by the guidelines of My word, then you are genuine disciples of Mine. And you will know the truth, and as a result, experience true freedom! (John 8:31-32).

Christ, Himself, is the One who designed His

spiritual body, and carefully fitted every part together in just the way He desired, so that every part, in its way, may function healthily by contributing to the rest of the body that which will strengthen and edify itself in love (Ephesians 4:16).

QUESTIONS TO PONDER

1. Is our local church grounded on the underlying principle of unconditional love? Are we really loving each other?

2. Is our church providing the freedom essential to spontaneous spiritual growth?

3. Is our church exercising biblical discipline?

4. Is our church providing an atmosphere of genuine fellowship characterized by love, acceptance, transparency, and supportive edification?

5. Is our church providing opportunities for each member to be a significant contribution to the rest of the body?

APPLICATION PROJECT

For the Church Leader and Lay Person

1. Rate the overall character of your church in general by circling the number which best describes the degree of each characteristic.

Loving	10	9	8	7	6	5	4	3	2	1	Self-centered
Joyful	10	9	8	7	6	5	4	3	2	1	Negativistic
Peaceful	10	9	8	7	6	5	4	3	2	1	Anxious
Patient	10	9	8	7	6	5	4	3	2	1	Impetuous
Kind	10	9	8	7	6	5	4	3	2	1	Quarrelsome
Generous	10	9	8	7	6	5	4	3	2	1	Selfish
Faithful	10	9	8	7	6	5	4	3	2	1	Undependable
Meek	10	9	8	7	6	5	4	3	2	1	Arrogant
Disciplined	10	9	8	7	6	5	4	3	2	1	Impulsive

2. Of the nine areas above, what are your church's three greatest strengths?
    a.
    b.
    c.
3. Of the nine areas above, what are your church's three greatest weaknesses?
    a.
    b.
    c.
4. What three specific steps can be taken to strengthen the above three weak areas?
    a.
    b.
    c.

5. Which spiritual gift(s) do you think the Holy Spirit has given you? (Circle the appropriate answer or answers.)
   a. Faith (praying)
   b. Teaching
   c. Helping
   d. Administering
   e. Exhorting
   f. Giving
   g. Showing mercy
   h. Evangelizing
   i. Pastoring
   j. Other

6. In what way are you presently utilizing your gift in your local church?

For the Church Leader Only

7. What opportunities is your church providing for spiritual ministry among its members?
8. What ministries could you delegate to elderly members, widows and young people who want to be engaged in the spiritual service of the church?

Elderly Members	Widows	Young People

9. Which of the following areas are shared at least in part by lay persons in the congregation:

   a. missionary contact
   b. visitation
   c. finances—budget
   d. education
   e. membership process
   f. benevolence
   g. mail exhortation
   h. mail evangelism
   i. outreach ministries
   j. administration
   k. counseling
   l. shepherding and discipleship

10. Draw up a questionnaire form which could be distributed to the members of your congregation polling their abilities and desires for ministry. (The following form is given as a sample. Notice the adaptation to regular visitors who may not yet be members. Use them! Perhaps their participation in the ministry will encourage them to join your team. At the same time, you will want to be sure of their doctrinal beliefs and convictions, depending on the type of service into which they are placed.)

SPIRITUAL SERVICE SURVEY

(Please complete this form and return to the Pastor or a Deacon)

Name_____ Date_____ Age_____ Sex_____

Address_____ Phone_____

How long a Christian?____ I am a member____, regular attender____, frequent visitor____, of this church for ____ years. Occupation_____.

(1) I believe my spiritual gift(s) to be the following (circle):

- a. Faith (praying)
- b. Teaching
- c. Helping (serving)
- d. Administrating
- e. Exhorting
- f. Giving
- g. Showing mercy
- h. Evangelizing
- i. Pastoring
- j. Other

(2) I believe my natural abilities to be the following:

- a. Singing
- b. Playing instrument_____
- c. Sports
- d. Academics
- e. Children's work
- f. Youth work
- g. Public relations
- h. Writing
- i. Public speaking
- j. Other

(3) My favorite hobbies include:

- a. Photography
- b. Arts & crafts
- c. Yard work
- d. Recording
- e. Camping
- f. Social sports
- g. Cooking/baking
- h. Correspondence
- i. Flower arranging
- j. Other

(4) Some of the skills which I have developed include:

- a. Typing
- b. Shorthand
- c. Calligraphy
- d. Accounting
- e. Filing
- f. Art
- g. Radio tech.
- h. Library sc.
- i. Plumbing
- j. Carpentry
- k. Handyman
- l. Other

(5) I would be willing to use my talents in the following capacities (please check):

____Specific Prayer Warrior
____Deacon
____Trustee

IS MY CHURCH WHAT GOD MEANT IT TO BE?

____Sunday School Teacher
____Children's Church Leader
____Awana Club Leader
____Home Bible Study Teacher
____Youth Sponsor
____Nursery Attendant
____Clerical Worker
____Pianist
____Organist
____Song Leader
____Choir Director
____Choir Member
____Vocal Soloist
____Instrumentalist
____Counselor
____Lay Preacher
____Evangelistic Correspondent
____Visitation Worker
____Member of the Education Committee
____Member of the Budget and Finance Committee
____Member of the Membership Committee
____Member of the Benevolence Committee
____Member of the Special Activities Committee
____Member of the Missionary Committee
____Member of the Ushers Committee
____Member of the Baptismal Committee
____Member of the Telephone Committee
____Member of the Nursery Committee
____Member of the Building & Grounds Committee
____Other:

4
Balancing
the Person

THE SWING OF THE PENDULUM

The twentieth century, with its divergent spectrum of Christian viewpoint, has also given rise to different contemporaneous church emphases as they relate to the members' individual development and welfare. With liberalism came the desire of its churches to develop the individual member of a church intellectually. The goal of many such churches was to teach their membership *how* to think—not *what* to think. Sadly enough, this too often involved the creative thinking of unregenerate minds. Hence the churches have reaped a harvest of much "qualitative" scholarship—but much of which was unscriptural and often antiscriptural.

With the 1940s came the birth of neo-evangelicalism. This movement of "concerned conservatives" not only endeavored to strive for a standard of excellence in the field of intellectual scholarship, but also purposed to effect a revival of *social* concern within the ranks of evangelicalism.

Despite their initially good intentions, it is again sad

but true that many churches of this stripe have emphasized social concern and intellectual excellence at the expense of maintaining a firm biblical position on areas of doctrine and other Christian responsibilities. On the other hand, many fundamental churches have been characterized by shallow thinking and social apathy, while trying to maintain the single goal of spiritual development in the individual.

Neo-orthodox churches tend to be uniquely aware of a person's emotional needs. And then, of course, there are those unique churches, complete with health food specialists, that are preoccupied with the physical needs of its members.

Which church is right? Should the church be more concerned for a believer's spiritual welfare, emotional welfare, or intellectual welfare; or should its concern be for the members' physical development—or social needs?

WHAT DID JESUS SAY?

In Mark 12:30, Jesus proclaimed, " 'And you shall love the Lord your God with all your heart, and with all your soul, and with all your mind, and with all your strength.' " Here is a stimulating command. A person is to demonstrate actively his genuine love for God *spiritually, emotionally, intellectually,* and *physically.* It goes without saying that if a person is to actively engage in demonstrating his genuine love to God in each of these areas, then he must necessarily strive to have a healthy heart, soul, mind and body.

This opens up an entirely revolutionary view of spiritual maturity. If I am to love God in each of these areas, then development and health in each of these areas is directly related to my spiritual maturity and well-being.

Since we stated earlier that the goal of the local church is to glorify God by presenting to Him believers that are both spiritually mature and reproductive, it can here be noted that in achieving that goal, it is therefore *also* the responsibility of the church to provide for the development and health of each member of the body intellectually, emotionally, physically, and socially. This, however, must be done in submission to and in accordance with the teaching of the Word of God.

FURTHER BIBLICAL INSTRUCTION

Jesus not only gave us a command—He also gave us an example! Dr. Luke reports, "And Jesus kept increasing in *wisdom* and *stature,* and *in favor with God* and *men*" (Luke 2:52, emphasis mine). Jesus Himself, in His incarnate state, developed intellectually, physically, spiritually, and socially. Christ's example is not limited to His own experience, but extends to His ministry as well. He did not stop with meeting a man's spiritual needs—He met the needs of the *whole man.* He ministered to *whole men.*

He healed the suffering body, provided food for the hungry, encouraged the troubled, taught the unlearned and gave new life to the dead spirit. Perhaps this is why the early apostolic church was so balanced in its ministry. The ministry of Jesus was still fresh in their minds.

Luke records the balance of the first local church in Jerusalem:

And they were continually devoting themselves to the apostles' teaching and to fellowship, to the breaking of bread and to prayer . . . And all those who had believed were together, and had all things in common; and they began selling their property

91

and possessions, and were sharing them with all, as anyone might have need. And day by day continuing with one mind in the temple, and breaking bread from house to house, they were taking their meals together with gladness and sincerity of heart, praising God, and having favor with all the people. And the Lord was adding to their number day by day those who were being saved (Acts 2:42,44-47).

PUTTING IT ALL TOGETHER

An Intellectual Being

God gave us minds to use. It is common knowledge that less than ten percent of our brain power is all that we usually use. Is this good stewardship? This might be understandable with an unregenerate mind, but the Christian has had his mind rejuvenated with the very life of God, Himself—the Creator and Organizer of the world!

Proverbs 10:14 declares, "Wise men store up knowledge." It is true that knowledge without the power of God's Spirit is in vain, but knowledge *with* the power of God's Spirit is God-honoring, and God's desire. Don't settle for sanctified ignorance when you can give God sanctified brain power.

The church should cultivate healthy thinking. Guided by obedience to the Word, the Christian should be challenged to be a creative thinker. He should not be a parasite to the pastor, but should know how to think for himself—how to discern, evaluate, and draw conclusions in every area of knowledge for himself.

All truth is God's truth. The Christian should *not* be guilty of limiting himself. He can gain much from and contribute much to the world of thought as it relates to the social sciences, modern literature, philosophy, education, astronomy, history, biology, anthropology, sociology, geology, archeology, science, music, psychology, and psychiatry. With the Spirit of God in control of our minds, there is no reason why we as Christians should take a back seat in the world of thought. We ought to be the leaders!

The principle for us to recognize here is the integration of truth. All truth is God's truth. This includes truth discovered by secular thinkers as well as truth proclaimed in the Scriptures. This can happen because God has chosen to reveal truth through general means as well as specific means. He reveals truth in nature, history, conscience and reason. However, since the Bible is the final authority of all truth, it is the standard and measuring rod by which all knowledge is tested.

Information which is in harmony with the Scriptures can therefore be utilized by the people of God and church of God. Dr. Kenneth Gangel states clearly:

> Since there is a God, and since that God has spoken in history, the most important aspect of learning for the Christian is to find out what God has said. God's revelation, both special and natural, becomes the heart and core of the curriculum.[1]

This means the church should be building a good and balanced library. It should keep itself informed with a good selection of regular periodicals. Reading can be promoted by perhaps a book of the month, or by posting worthy articles.

The church should also make use of information gleaned outside of special revelation which remains consistent with it. For example, principles of psychology can be used in counseling. Principles of administration can be used in the Sunday School.

May God grant to the local church the desire to cultivate the minds of its disciples.

An Emotional Being

Hershey and Lugo report in *Living Psychology:*

> At least 1 person in every 10 (19 million in all) has some form of mental illness (from mild to severe) . . . At least 50% of all the medical and surgical cases treated by private doctors and hospitals have a mental illness complication. Over 1,500,000 persons are hospitalized for mental illness during the year. On any one day of the year about 760,000 persons are under psychiatric care of hospitals.[2]

It is complete naivete which believes that a Christian is free from emotional needs and emotional conflicts. The Bible is full of recorded incidents of believers who suffered emotional conflict. David fought depression (Psalm 42:5,6,11); Noah sought escape from his loneliness by resorting to alcohol (Genesis 9:21); Jonah and Elijah—both called men of God—seriously considered suicide (1 Kings 19:4; Jonah 1:12; 4:3), and Paul refers to several believers who had definite breakdowns in interpersonal relationships.

There are a number of events in the Scriptures which reveal the neurotic battles of repression, displacement, projection, suppression, rationalization, escapism, sadism, masochism, and melancholia. Why? Men are emotional beings—and emotional beings have emotional needs and conflicts.

I recently taught a course in Christian Psychology to one hundred and forty Christian laypeople from various local churches. I consider these men and women to be among the cream of the crop. Nevertheless, many severe problems surfaced as I met with them individually. After each student took the Taylor-Johnson Temperament Analysis, some basic observations could be made. There is a direct relationship between spiritual growth and emotional stability. However, it became also apparent that even the most dedicated Christians can and do experience serious emotional problems.

Yes, even in the best local churches you will find individuals wrestling with guilt, hostility, depression, suicidal tendencies, sexual conflicts, marital conflicts, anxiety. Why? All of us are human beings, and every human being is an emotional being.

God is very concerned about the emotional health of His people. For this reason, there are multiplied hundreds of verses in the Holy Scriptures which directly deal with man's emotional needs and conflicts. The Book of Proverbs is perhaps the most concentrated section of the Bible on this particular area of man's needs. Jesus Himself desired that His disciples become consistently happy and healthy personalities: "These things I have spoken to you, that My joy may be in you, and that your joy may be made full" (John 15:11).

In his book, *The Mental Health Ministry of the Local Church,* Howard Clinebell, Jr. states:

> (a) Mental health is a central and inescapable concern of any local church that is a healing-redemptive fellowship. (b) A local church today has an unprecedented opportunity to multiply its contributions to both the preventive and the therapeutic dimensions

of mental health. (c) A church can seize this opportunity most effectively by allowing mental health to become a leavening concern, permeating all areas of its life.[3]

There are several measures that a local church can take in caring for the emotional development and health of the members:

(a) Use the pulpit for public counseling as it directly relates to the exposition and application of the Word of God. A church in Dallas just completed a series of Sunday evening messages on the emotional problems of loneliness, depression, fear, anxiety and guilt. Each message was Bible-centered and specifically dealt with the heart of each need. Psychologists teach the steps to mental health as the acceptance of oneself, the acceptance of others, and the acceptance of circumstances. The Bible goes even deeper! The Bible promises joy to those who view themselves as God does—cleansed, gifted and loved; to those who view others as God does—needy and loved; and to those who view circumstances as God does—designed by God for their ultimate good (Romans 8:28). Many of these principles can be shared from the church pulpit.

(b) Provide qualitative pastoral counseling. The pastor should be equipped to handle the more common emotional needs and conflicts of his people. It will not do to just say, "Let's pray about it." God has already given to us the principles of emotional health through natural and biblical revelation. He expects us to learn them and use them. Prepare to counsel and then let the people know that you are available.

(c) Cultivate a healthy church "group life" that will provide the atmosphere for healthy interpersonal relationships. Co-ed teenage functions may decrease adolescent tendencies toward homosexuality and masturbation. Functions for the senior citizens will restore their feelings of worth and self-esteem. Church "family functions" will strengthen the communication and relationships within the Christian home.

(d) Train laymen in the field of Christian counseling. Simple principles can be shared with them, who, in turn, can share them with others.

A Physical Being

The Word of God and the God of the Word are both concerned with the physical health and the well-being of man. In the Old Testament law, God endeavored to keep his people from doing those things that would bring harm to the body. This included laws concerning food and drink as well as bodily activity. In the New Testament, Jesus Christ was actively engaged in a healing ministry which not only revealed His deity, but also revealed His concern for the physical needs of man. His ministry not only included a healing program, but also a preventative program which included the feeding of the hungry. Later Paul exhorts the believer to take care of his body for it is the temple of the Holy Spirit. He even admits the profit of physical exercise.

Medical doctor S. I. McMillen in his book, *None of These Diseases,* gives case after case of a biblical principle of physical health which has been discovered and utilized in the world of medicine.[4] C. S. Lovett, in *Jesus Wants You Well,* presents the "healing laws" which God built into the body complex and the world of nature.[5] Two of those laws, which seem so commonplace and yet are so very vital to good health are physical exercise and the balanced diet. Concerning exercise he writes:

> Christians who do not exercise their bodies have
> thousands of collapsed capillaries. Sedentary ones
> have unbelievable numbers of them completely out
> of action. The result is that millions of the body cells
> are denied food and oxygen, to say nothing of the
> waste materials allowed to accumulate. With so
> many cells undernourished, these people become
> sluggish. Their vital organs become subject to
> disease. They may eat balanced meals, but they still
> suffer poor health.[6]

One might ask the question, "How can one who is in
poor physical condition serve God?" The answer may
well be stated, "To be sure, anyone can serve God, but no
one can deny that the better condition a person is in, the
more pleasantly and the more effectively he will be able to
serve."

Psychiatrist Marion H. Nelson devotes a whole chapter
to the "Physical Causes of Nervous Tensions" in his
book, *Why Christians Crack Up.* He concludes by saying:

> Christians frequently do not realize how much their
> spiritual outlook is affected by their physical condi-
> tion. It is hard to feel and act spiritual when one is
> physically ill. So we must correct anything wrong
> with us in order to operate at the highest peak
> spiritually.[7]

Examples abound. According to Dr. Paul Meier, an
individual whose diet excludes protein "may become
anemic and more irritable and rebellious."[8] One who
overeats may also struggle with "increased feelings of

guilt and loss of self-esteem,'' plus an increased chance of heart attack with its correspondent anxieties.[9] A lack of sleep can also have spiritual implications. "Going without sleep for two or three days, many normal people will begin to exhibit psychotic tendencies, such as delusions and paranoid ideation.[10]

Spiritual and emotional conflicts can also be seen in many suffering from hyperactivity, hypoglycemia, hyperthyroidism, mononucleosis, physical stress, and old age, as documented by Dr. Frank Minirth.[11] So, then, our physical health is basic to our emotional and spiritual health in many ways.

As a matter of fact, we have seen that proper care of the body alone is one way of demonstrating our love to God, for we are stewards of the body which He has given to us and which is now the temple of God Himself. Lovett continues:

> Look around you. Do you see Christians anywhere near the peak of health? Rarely. Most have allowed their vitality to slip away. They haven't noticed it, perhaps, but it was steadily taking place. How many do you know who have the vigor, the bounce, the snap that accompanies buoyant health? Who in your church exhibits the zip, the pep, the effervescence, the GLOW of perfect health? You just don't see it. Oh yes, the people are alive and move around, but you don't see the bounce that comes from radiant, good health. It just isn't there—except in the very young.[12]

The balanced church, then, is one that not only looks after the intellectual and emotional needs of the people, but the physical needs as well. Some churches are located in poverty belts with some families who rarely enjoy a well-balanced meal. The church should be vitally concerned to the point of action.

Other churches are located within the center of a community that is preoccupied in the business world and greatly in need of physical exercise. Such a church would do well to carry on a recreational ministry for its members. Instruction could be given in the church school in areas of personal hygiene and fitness. The pastoral staff should serve as an example and an encouragement to its people. The pastor should know of a good physician whom he can recommend to his people.

A bulletin board can be placed in the church building which will periodically remind people to get a chest X ray or flu shot or to have their blood pressure checked. If Christ was so keenly concerned about the physical well-being of His people, we should be the same.

A Social Being

As a social being, man is capable of building interpersonal relationships and adjustments to society. The skill of relating to people is a Christian mandate (Mark 12:31). How sad it is, then, to find antisocial Christians. That very term is self-contradictory, yet the reality exists.

The Diagnostic and Statistical Manual of Mental Disorders describes antisocial individuals as those:

> . . . who are basically unsocialized and whose behavior pattern brings them repeatedly into conflict with society. They are incapable of significant loyalty to individuals, groups or social values. They are grossly selfish, callous, irresponsible, impulsive, and unable to feel guilt or to learn from experience and punishment. Frustration tolerance is low. They

tend to blame others or offer plausible rationalizations for their behavior.[13]

I had a friend whose constant cry was "interpersonal relationships." That's all he ever talked about. Yet he himself was not able to relate to other individuals. He merely projected his inability onto everyone else. Was he a believer? Yes.

There seem to be six foundational principles in the Scriptures basic to the ability to relate to others: (1) acknowledge your own depravity, Romans 3:19; (2) admit your weaknesses and mistakes, Galatians 6:1-3; (3) agree to disagree, 2 Timothy 2:23-25; (4) accept others, John 13:34; (5) act responsibly, 1 Thessalonians 5:21-22; and (6) allow for failure, 1 John 3:2.

The local church should provide opportunities for the development of social skills. Church socials, youth parties, Sunday School picnics, men's softball teams and various types of get-togethers can be most rewarding to everyone.

However, the believer's social expression should not be limited to the church. The individual member of the local church is not isolated from the world—and he should not be. True, it is not God's will that he be "*of* the world," but it *is* God's plan that he be "*in* the world." His responsibility does not revolve merely around the church. His interpersonal relationships are not limited to believers. He has a job, lives in a neighborhood, is a citizen of a community, and meets people every day in the common chores relative to living in the twentieth century. He does not live on an island.

How does he relate to members of other local churches with whom he may disagree? Is he threatened? Is he afraid? Does he feel inferior? Or does he feel superior—"holier-than-thou"? What is his responsibility to the needs of society? Is he apathetic? Indifferent? Jesus said, "You are the salt of the earth . . . You are the light of the world" (Matthew 5:13-14a).

Paul told Timothy that a servant of God "must have a good reputation with those outside the church" (1 Timothy 3:7a). He told the Galatians, "While we have opportunity, let us do good to all men" (Galatians 6:10a). And once again Jesus said, " 'You shall love your neighbor as yourself' " (Mark 12:31b).

To be a balanced believer, one must know how to "get along with" the world. True, he must *never* forsake his Christian holiness, but he must learn—as Christ practiced—to love the unholy, care for the unholy, and win the unholy.

The balanced church, then, is a local fellowship that fosters the ability to love, relate and to care for the world and its members. It is a church that develops Christians who are conformed to the image of Christ—not the image of the Pharisee—when it comes to understanding and caring for those who have not yet received the blessing of salvation. One man put it this way: "I view myself as being merely a satisfied beggar telling other beggars where to find the bread."

Despite the accusations of new evangelicals, fundamentalists are not against social concern. What fundamentalists are opposed to is a social gospel. Unfortunately, this is usually where the new evangelical preoccupation with social concern ends. Richard Quebedeaux boldly states in *The Young Evangelicals:*

It is in this spirit that the Young Evangelicals espouse a truly Evangelical Social Gospel—one that meets the deepest needs of the heart and the urgent demands of society in turmoil as well. Their new values and ethics—motivated by a biblical faith and a rich understanding of the meaning of discipleship—are best reflected in the fresh priorities of these young men and women which include: (1) sexual love as a joyful experience; (2) meaningful interpersonal and social relationships and the dignity of women; (3) racial justice; (4) the politics of conscience; (5) the fight against poverty; (6) a healthy natural environment; and (7) a positive and happy participation in contemporary culture.[14]

Many fundamentalists, on the other hand, are truly desirous of genuine biblical social concern, while recognizing that it is not the gospel itself or even part of the gospel but an expression of the love of God which is a result of the gospel as well as a means of making it known.

Jackson, writing in behalf of the Regular Baptist Movement, stated:

God forbid that we should be lacking in compassion toward the needy. With acts of love we can melt many hearts that have remained as flint under the preaching of truth. But may we never forget that without the truth, even a melted heart can never be saved![15]

With objective perspective, Robert Lightner summarizes the issue:

The social concern of neo-evangelicalism is not new nor is it wrong. It only becomes wrong when interest in social sins takes precedence over the need of individual redemption, when the application of the message takes priority over the gospel itself.[16]

The balanced believer does not erase "social concern" from his practical vocabulary. His active concern for the needs of society, however, is kept in balance with the other areas of Christian living and responsibility. It is not his constant cry. It is a sensitive awareness which joins the other facets of his Christian experience.

A Spiritual Being

The believer is commanded in Ephesians 5:18 to "be filled with the Spirit." While the spirit of the unregenerate man is dead and inoperative, the spirit of the believer is given new life—and that life is to be controlled by the Spirit of God.

Spirituality has often been sincerely misunderstood. In short, when a believer is spiritual, he is manifesting the fruit of the Spirit. Galatians 5:22-23 describes the fruit of the Spirit as being love, joy, peace, patience, kindness, goodness, faithfulness, gentleness, and self-control. This "fruit" of the Spirit is contrasted to the "works" of the flesh. This is significant. The fruit of the Spirit is NOT something which WE produce—it is something which GOD produces.

We are not, however, free from responsibility, for we are told that in order to bear fruit, we must ABIDE IN THE VINE! In the work of sanctification, then, we are to do our part (abide in the vine), and God will do His part (produce spiritual fruit). Jesus Christ Himself is the vine: "Abide in Me, and I in you. As the branch cannot bear fruit of itself, unless it abides in the vine, so neither can you, unless you abide in Me. I am the vine, you are the branches; he who abides in Me, and I in him, he bears much fruit; for apart from Me you can do nothing" (John 15:4-5).

Abiding in Christ is explained in the following verses as being accomplished by abiding in His Word (by knowing it and doing it) and by abiding in prayer. As we let Him speak to us through His Word, and as we speak to Him in prayer, we will begin to resemble Him in our conduct—for the fruit of the Spirit is nothing less than the characteristics of Jesus Christ. This merely involves the age-old principle that a man becomes like those with whom he spends most of his time.

My wife is from the South. I am from the North. On our first date at Moody Bible Institute our accents were as different as night and day. We almost needed a translator! Today, several years later, my accent is heavily southern flavored, and my wife's is northern flavored. Why the change? We take on the characteristics of those with whom we associate the most. That is why teenagers are warned to pick their close friends carefully—especially at that formative age.

Jesus Christ is unchangeable. If we abide in Him through His Word and prayer, we will begin to take on His characteristics (not His attributes). This is spirituality. Our responsibility is actively (not passively) to yield our lives to Him.

A word of caution needs to be sounded concerning the study of the Word of God as it relates to spiritual growth. Ryrie warns:

> There are two extremes to be avoided in one's use of the Bible in sanctification. The one might be labeled spiritual schizophrenia which is a "type of psychosis characterized by loss of contact with environment and by disintegration of personality." In other

words, the spiritual schizophrenic is the person who never allows the Bible to make contact with the life situation in which he finds himself. His orthodoxy is without reproach but his orthopraxy leaves a lot to be desired. Or in the words of Scripture he is a hearer and not a doer of the Word. His knowledge of the Word is not integrated with his habits of living. We must never disunite doctrine from practice.[17]

The other extreme to be avoided in one's use of the Bible is mysticism. Pseudospiritual people are often afflicted with this. Some of the symptoms are: "The Lord led me not to go to church;" "The Lord gave me such a wonderful thought this morning out of such-and-such a verse"—a thought which, upon examining the verse, is nowhere to be found. "I don't need anyone to teach me the Bible—the Holy Spirit is the only teacher I need." Of course, the Holy Spirit does teach us the meaning of the Word, and His ministry is indispensable (John 16:13; 1 Corinthians 2:12). But the Bible does not say that His ministry of teaching will always be direct. Indeed, it is most often mediated through gifted teachers of the past and present whom God has given to the church. Sometimes this ministry may be direct as one persistently and intelligently searches out the meaning of a passage. But often it comes through the pastor's message or the teacher's lesson or a concordance or other books of men both living and dead.[18]

In other words, the believer should be challenged to study the objective Word of God *inductively* and systematically. After he understands the meaning of the passage of Scripture, he should then endeavor to put it into practice for himself. This process, coupled with prayer, is the life-source of spirituality. The local church should be the guiding force which continually motivates, instructs, and encourages true spirituality.

Getting the total picture, the individual members of the local body of believers are seen to have intellectual, emotional, physical, social and spiritual capacities. Christ was concerned about the development and health of the total man. The balanced Christian church is also concerned about the development and health of every area of life for each of its members.

PUTTING IT INTO PARAPHRASE

Demonstrate your love for the Lord your God in every area of life—spiritually, emotionally, intellectually, and physically (Mark 12:30).

And Jesus developed intellectually, physically, spiritually, and socially (Luke 2:52).

APPLICATION PROJECT

For the Church Leader and Lay Person

1. Concerning intellectual development, answer the following true and false questions.
    a. (T/F) Our church encourages creative thinking.
    b. (T/F) Our church is characterized by knowledge integration.
    c. (T/F) Our church is developing a church library.
    d. (T/F) Our church tolerates minor differences of intellectual opinion.
    e. (T/F) Our church is concerned with quality education.
2. Get acquainted with available resources in the area of emotional growth and counseling. Here is a very limited list to whet your appetite.

Books

Christian Psychology

Collins, Gary, *Search For Reality* (Wheaton, IL: Key Publishers, 1969)

Minirth, Frank, *Christian Psychiatry* (Old Tappan, NJ: Fleming H. Revell Company, 1977)

Narramore, Clyde M., *Encyclopedia of Psychological Problems* (Grand Rapids: Zondervan Publishing House, 1976)

Nelson, Marion H., *Why Christians Crack Up* (Chicago: Moody Press, 1974)

Child Psychology & Personality Development

Benson, Clarence H., *Understanding Children and Youth* (Wheaton, IL: Evangelical Teacher Training Association, 1969)

Hadfield, J. A., *Childhood & Adolescence* (Baltimore: Penguin Books, 1970)

Meier, Paul D., *Christian Child-Rearing and Personality Development* (Grand Rapids: Baker Book House, 1977)

Winter, Gerald D. and Eugene M. Nuss, *Young Adult, The* (Glenview, IL: Scott, Foresman and Company, 1969)

Christian Marriage and Family

Clinebell, Howard J. and Charlotte H., *The Intimate Marriage* (New York: Harper & Row, Publishers, 1970)

Hendricks, Howard G., *Heaven Help the Home* (Wheaton: Victor Books, 1973)

Mace, David R., *Getting Ready For Marriage* (Nashville: Abingdon Press, 1972)

Wright, H. Norman, *Communication: Key To Your Marriage* (Glendale, CA: G/L Publications, 1974)

Counseling

Adams, Jay E., *The Christian Counselor's Manual* (Philadelphia: Presbyterian and Reformed Publishing Company, 1973)

Crabb, Lawrence J., *Effective Biblical Counseling* (Grand Rapids: Zondervan Publishing House, 1977)

Crane, William E., *Where God Comes In* (Waco: Word Books, 1970)

Walvoord, John E., ed. *Christian Counseling For Contemporary Problems* (Dallas: Dallas Theological Seminary, n.d.)

Counseling Materials

a. *The Christian Counselor's Starter Packet*
Prepared by Dr. Jay Adams
c/o Presbyterian & Reformed Publishing
   Company
Box 185
Nutley, NJ 07110

b. *The Taylor-Johnson Temperament Analysis Kit*
c/o Psychological Publications, Inc.
5300 Hollywood Boulevard
Los Angeles, CA 90027

c. Various counseling kits and tests are available from:
Family Life Publications, Inc.
Saluda, NC 28773

d. Helpful tapes are available from:
Christian Marriage Enrichment
1070 Detroit St.
Denver, CO 80206

Informational Resources

American Association of Christian Counselors
3912 Marian Avenue
Memphis, TN 38111

Christian Counseling Centers

Find the location of the one nearest your church.

3. Which of these physical ministries could be implemented in your church?
   a. Youth recreational program (yes/no)
   b. A camping ministry (yes/no)

   c. Winter or summer retreats (yes/no)
   d. Church softball teams (yes/no)
   e. Food basket ministry (yes/no)
   f. Bulletin board reminders (yes/no)
   g. List of recommended physicians and specialists (yes/no)
   h. Sex counseling on tape for married couples (yes/no) (Example: *Sex Techniques & Sex Problems in Marriage* by Dr. Ed Wheat, 130 Spring, Springdale, AR 72764)

4. a. Sit down with your family and objectively evaluate the social strengths and weaknesses of your church, your family, and yourself as an individual.
   b. Adjust the following sentences:
    —I am/am not an inhibited person.
    —I am/am not a quiet person.
    —I am/am not a hostile person.
    —I am/am not an indifferent person.
    —I am/am not a tolerant person.
    —I am/am not a submissive person.
    —I am/am not a consistently happy person.
    —I am/am not a rigid person.

5. Rate your own spiritual character by circling the number which best describes the degree of each characteristic. Be honest.

Self-centered	1	2	3	4	5	6	7	8	9	10	Loving
Negative	1	2	3	4	5	6	7	8	9	10	Joyful
Anxious	1	2	3	4	5	6	7	8	9	10	Peaceful
Impetuous	1	2	3	4	5	6	7	8	9	10	Patient
Quarrelsome	1	2	3	4	5	6	7	8	9	10	Kind

Selfish	1	2	3	4	5	6	7	8	9	10	Generous
Undependable	1	2	3	4	5	6	7	8	9	10	Faithful
Arrogant	1	2	3	4	5	6	7	8	9	10	Meek
Impulsive	1	2	3	4	5	6	7	8	9	10	Disciplined

6. Commit those areas that need refinement to the Lord in prayer and begin a positive plan for growth in those areas.

5
Balancing
the Pastor

THE SWING OF THE PENDULUM

I was in a church a couple of years ago where the pastor boldly came to the pulpit and said arrogantly, "The board has made a decision to follow this course of action. By the way, *I am the church board.*"

What he said was absolutely true—*he* was the governing "board" of that church. No one dared contradict his word, for he ruled the church.

Just recently I heard the testimony of another minister relating the experience of his first pastorate. He told the congregation he would only accept the call to be their pastor under one condition—he would be the dictator of that church. Unfortunately—they called him. This style of leadership is not uncommon in today's evangelical world and is rightly labeled, "the autocratic style."

On the other hand, I recall serving on the staff of a church whose pastor—sweet man of God that he was—was just the opposite. His never-dying question was, "What should I do?" At the same time, he let every other officer of the church call his own shots and brought every administrative question to the congregation without a sense of direction.

This "laissez-faire" style of leadership is also common in today's church world. Which is the most biblical? Let's take a look at Jesus' leadership style.

WHAT DID JESUS DO?

Perhaps John 10 best illustrates the leadership style of the Lord Jesus:

> "But he who enters by the door is a shepherd of the sheep. To him the doorkeeper opens, and the sheep hear his voice, and he calls his own sheep by name, and leads them out. When he puts forth all his own, he goes before them, and the sheep follow him because they know his voice . . . I am the good shepherd; the good shepherd lays down His life for the sheep . . . I am the good shepherd; and I know My own, and My own know Me" (John 10:2-4,11,14).

FURTHER BIBLICAL INSTRUCTION

Later, Peter writes, addressing himself to pastors (elders) in 1 Peter 5:2-4 saying:

> Shepherd the flock of God among you, not under compulsion, but voluntarily, according to the will of God; and not for sordid gain, but with eagerness; nor yet as lording it over those allotted to your charge, but proving to be examples to the flock. And when the Chief Shepherd appears, you will receive the unfading crown of glory.

What a beautiful style of leadership this is! In both the

example of our Lord and the exhortation of Peter, we see what is to comprise pastoral leadership. The picture is neither one of the autocratic nor the laissez-faire. It is, however, that perfect blend of superintending guidance and sacrificial love. This is the "shepherd style" of leadership.

It is interesting to note the psychological building blocks of a leader's personality. A person doesn't just decide what kind of leader he is going to be. He is molded by his experiences. This molding and building process begins early in his childhood. I recall hearing one pastor say that he had always been a failure. He tried out for the football team but didn't make it. He strove for academic excellence—but just didn't make it. This was his story in just about every area of life. He began to acquire a persecution complex, feeling that everyone was down on him because they underestimated (or correctly estimated) his abilities.

One day he introduced a person to Christ. "Here is finally something I can do!" he thought excitedly. From that day on, he has had the burning desire to be the pastor of the most influential and largest church in America. It should be no surprise to the reader that this is the same pastor referred to earlier who stated that *he* was the church board. It is not for us to judge whether his current zeal in the ministry is a spiritual vision or a psychological defense mechanism—however, it should cause each of us to do some heart searching and examine our own motives honestly.

Oddly enough, many of the laissez-faire style of leadership are also molded by similar circumstances. A few have confided in me that they are still suffering guilt feelings from mistakes they made or sins they committed years and years ago which have long since been forgiven and forgotten by the Lord. However, instead of building up their own self-ego by establishing a strong pulpit (as in the example above), they continue on in their feelings of inferiority and therefore feel unworthy of bearing any authority over others.

An inferiority complex can have devastating effects upon one's ministry. Shaffer and Shoben list the traits of an inferiority complex as *sensitiveness to criticism, ideas of reference* "in which a person applies all criticism to himself," *seclusiveness, over-response to flattery, poor reaction to competition* and a *tendency to derogate others.*[1]

How many pastors have you seen with these marks? I can think of many, unfortunately. And how do they operate under these traits? They usually employ an excess of defense mechanisms—compensation, rationalization, projection, reaction formation and others. Shafer and Shoben cite a case discussed by Morgan who:

. . . described a young clergyman whose sermons developed into frenzied tirades against sin, which to him was synonymous with anything suggesting sexual conduct. He alienated his congregation by denunciation of dancing, new styles of dressing or of hair arrangement, cosmetics, and vice, which he considered all in the same category. He forbade the boys and girls of his congregation to walk home from church together. This young man was trying to live a celibate life which he believed essential to his calling. His quite normal sexual impulses and thoughts aroused severe anxiety in him, which he controlled by strengthening his defenses against any evidence of sex in others.[2]

So instead of dealing with his own feelings, he projected them onto others. Such is the state of the insecure pastor. In a sense, then, the roots of both extremes in leadership style are the same.

These feelings are difficult to unlearn. Both types of leaders ought to bring their situations under the careful scrutiny of the Word of God and seek the counsel of other wise counselors who will be able to help them objectively. The point is this—the pastor should strive for a healthy leadership which is biblical in philosophy.

The pastor of the New Testament church was a balanced pastor. He was a guide, but one who sought the desires of the congregation. He knew how to make the necessary pastoral decisions, but gave the congregation the right and privilege of making its own major decisions. He worked *with* the people, not *over* the people as their lord.

In speaking of confident pastoral leadership, Sugden and Wiersbe remind us:

You do not *demand* respect; you *command* it. Your people want to love you and follow you, but they need time to get to know you. Once you have won their love and respect, they will be willing to follow your leadership. Quietly go to work winning the lost, organizing the work, building the saints, and moving the church into wider ministries; and in time, God's blessing will win for you the respect and cooperation you desire.[3]

In connection with this discussion on the balanced pastor, I would like to mention three dangers which seek to ruin an effective ministry.[4]

IS MY CHURCH WHAT GOD MEANT IT TO BE?

Pastoral Image

I recall my battle with this problem during my first year in the pastorate. It was my fourth funeral and I was sitting in the home of the bereaved widow just moments following the memorial service. I recall that while sitting there I asked myself the question over and over again, "Now, how should a *pastor* act?" After getting a mental picture of the pastoral image, I turned off my own personality and squeezed myself into the "pastoral mold." I was no longer myself. I was acting a role—an acceptable one to be sure—nevertheless, I was wearing a facade. In a few minutes it dawned on me that my dear sister in Christ had some vital needs, and the least important of all things was *my image!*

My victory was short-lived. Constantly, I lived and ministered under the pressure of pastoral image. "How should a minister act? What should a minister say?" My inner life was one of a constant struggle with guilt for I was not free to be myself and act according to the spontaneity of the Holy Spirit's directions. My constant concern was to play the accepted role of the minister. Not only was I cheating my people and frustrating myself, but quenching the Holy Spirit as well.

Ministerial Machinery

The second danger I struggled with in those early years was strong devotion to ministerial machinery. I was more interested in my library, my office, my filing system, and my pulpit than I was in *people!* It was as though the ministry itself had become my god! I was insensitive to the real needs of my people. I was always busy—very busy—but in the machinery, not in lives. I did not empathetically weep with those who wept and laugh with those who laughed. I was just too busy.

Professional Pride

The third danger is the next logical step in such a sequence—professional pride in the pastorate. I often had to ask myself the question, "Is Jesus using me, or am I using Jesus?" Yes, I tried to make every message homiletically exciting, hermeneutically accurate, and exegetically sound. There was one problem: Was I preaching because I really wanted to meet the needs of my people—or did I want (maybe just a little bit) to impress them with my "great gift" of oratory?

Was I concerned only about what they thought of the Lord when I was through, or was I concerned (maybe just a little bit) with what they thought about the preacher? If only then I would have read the words of Charles Spurgeon who said:

Earnestness in the pulpit must be real. It is not to be mimicked. We have seen it counterfeited, but every person with a grain of sense could detect the imposition. To stamp the foot, to smite the desk, to perspire, to shout, to bawl, to quote the pathetic portions of other people's sermons, or to pour out voluntary tears from a watery eye will never make up for true agony of soul and real tenderness of spirit. The best piece of acting is but acting; those who only look at appearances may be pleased by it, but lovers of reality will be disgusted. What a presumption!—what hypocrisy it is by skillful management of the voice to mimic the passion which is the genuine work of the Holy Ghost. Let mere actors beware, lest they be found sinning against the

Holy Spirit by their theatrical performances.[5]

How many others have told me that their biggest temptation was to use the ministry for the sake of their own success and popularity! No, these were not phonies—just God-called men who were being honest about their real temptations.

I am reminded of the words of Jerome cited by St. Thomas Aquinas in *Summa Theologica*, "Shun, as you would the plague, a cleric who from being poor has become wealthy, or who, from being a nobody has become a celebrity."[6]

Well do I remember the proud feeling I had when, shortly after ordination, I put "Rev." on our mailbox in the front yard. How interesting to note that perhaps the greatest theologian of church history, St. Augustine, remarked, "For it is grace alone that separates the redeemed from the lost."[7] Indeed, even the most influential pastor of church history was merely a sinner saved by grace.

These are three severe dangers—but they are not without divine antidotes. In place of pastoral image, God tells us to be *ourselves*. In place of preoccupation with ministerial machinery, God tells us to *love people*. In place of professional pride, God tells us to *recognize our weakness and His grace*.

Perhaps there is no better example of a servant of God who successfully avoided these dangers than that of the Apostle Paul in 1 Corinthians 1:27-2:5:

But God has chosen the foolish things of the world to shame the wise, and God has chosen the weak things of the world to shame the things which are strong, and the base things of the world and the despised, God has chosen, the things that are not, that He might nullify the things that are, that no man should boast before God. But by His doing you are in Christ Jesus, who became to us wisdom from God, and righteousness and sanctification, and redemption, that, just as it is written, "Let him who boasts, boast in the Lord."

And when I came to you, brethren, I did not come with superiority of speech or of wisdom, proclaiming to you the testimony of God. For I determined to know nothing among you except Jesus Christ, and Him crucified. And I was with you in weakness and in fear and in much trembling. And my message and my preaching were not in persuasive words of wisdom, but in demonstration of the Spirit and of power, that your faith should not rest on the wisdom of men, but on the power of God.

PUTTING IT ALL TOGETHER

The balanced pastor is not an autocratic dictator over the local body of believers. Neither is he irresponsible and backward with respect to leadership. He is, however, a man of conviction who leads the flock by a loving example and balanced superintendence. He is a man who is genuine, compassionate, and humble — yet strong in character.

In view of the extreme importance of the scriptural qualifications for the pastor as found in 1 Timothy and Titus, Getz held a discussion with a group of Christian men in order to determine the practical implications of such standards. Concerning the principle of 1 Timothy 3:2a, "An overseer, then, must be above reproach," the group gave this list of characteristics which would identify the man who, in their opinion, meets this qualification:

He is a lovable guy!
He is honest; I'd trust him with my bank account!
He is a sensitive person!
He radiates Christ!
He is a good father!
He loves people — his wife, his family, everybody!
He works hard!
He sure is a humble guy!
He keeps his word!
He is not self-centered or conceited!
He makes you feel comfortable!
I can recommend him for most any task!
He doesn't let you down!
He won't take advantage of you!
He is not an opportunist!
He doesn't use people for his own ends!
He knows where he's going; he plans ahead!
He is thoughtful and cordial!
He is fair!
He is a good steward of time and talent!
He doesn't lose his cool!
He is consistent!
He recognizes and respects authority!
He hangs in there and perseveres!
He admits when he is wrong!
He is teachable!
He doesn't have a martyr complex!
He is an honest person!
You know what he is thinking![8]

This is a very convicting list for the average pastor—
myself included. But with the help of God, may each of
us who carry any responsibility in the work of Christ

strive for nothing less than these necessary qualities.

PUTTING IT INTO PARAPHRASE

But he who comes in the door of the sheepfold is the shepherd himself. The doorkeeper will open the door for him and the sheep respectfully and lovingly hear his voice; and he calls each of his own sheep by their names, and leads them on. He continues this process by going before them as an example, and the sheep follow him, because they know him in an intimate way. Jesus said, "I am the good shepherd. The good shepherd sacrifices his own life for the sake of the sheep. I am the good shepherd, and I know My own, and My own know Me" (John 10:2-4,11,14).

Shepherd the flock of God over whom you are the leader, not because you are forced to, but because you really want to; not for selfish reasons, but eagerly for the right reasons. Don't be a dictator to these beloved believers, but guide them by being an example. And when the Chief Pastor appears, you will, as a result, be rewarded by the unfading crown of glory which you will later cast at His feet in worship (1 Peter 5:2-4; cf. Revelation 4:11).

APPLICATION PROJECT

For the Pastor

1. Put a check beside the name which best describes you:
   a. Pastor Paranoid (sensitive, suspicious)
   b. Rev. Updown (easily excited or depressed)
   c. Shy Shepherd (reserved, withdrawn)
   d. Holy Hothead (explosive, hostile)
   e. Doctor Dictator (domineering, self-centered)
   f. Preacher Screecher (dramatic, emotional)
   g. Theo Theologue (meticulous, rigid)
   h. Brother Boulder (stubborn, procrastinator)
   i. Saint Sickly (hypochondriacal, easily fatigued)
   j. Parson Pancake (inadequate, no stamina)
2. What are the assets of your pastoral personality? List at least three.
   a.
   b.
   c.
3. What are the liabilities of your pastoral personality?
   a.
   b.
   c.

For the Church Member

1. Before you think too much about your pastor's personality profile, take a look at yourself. In light of this chapter, what kind of potential leader are you?
   a. Autocratic
   b. Laissez-faire
   c. Balanced

2. Describe *your* personality in 50 words or less (touching both strengths and weaknesses).

_____

_____

_____

_____

_____

3. I will pray regularly for my pastor, that God will use his strengths and refine his weaknesses in God's good time. Yes/No.

For Everyone

1. Sit down with someone you deeply respect and ask him/her to give you an objective evaluation of your leadership. Listen carefully. Use this as a choice opportunity to be stretched in your personal growth.
2. If possible, take a personality inventory such as the Minnesota Multiphasic Personality Inventory or the Taylor-Johnson Temperament Analysis. These are available through your local Christian Counseling Centers.
3. Getz' book, *Measure of a Man,* is an excellent tool for personal growth. You may want to work through it with a group of others or by yourself. It is listed in the bibliography.

6
Balancing
the Pulpit

THE SWING OF THE PENDULUM

In chapters one and two, we discussed balance as it relates to edification and evangelism, stating that the early church was equally involved in both. We continued to illustrate, however, that it was the church "dispersed" which was engaged in evangelism, and the church "assembled" which engaged in edification. At this point in our discussion, then, we must raise the question, "What shall we preach to the assembled believers in order that they might be edified?" Once again, there are two basic extremes which we find today in many of our local churches.

On the one hand, there are those well-meaning preachers whose ministry is essentially comprised of exhortation. They are known for their "sermonic" messages. They continually scold the saints for the things which they are doing wrong, and/or they are continually telling the saints what they should do that they are not now doing.

To make it look "scriptural," there is usually a story

from the Bible tacked on for good measure, and a tricky alliterated outline, giving the usually false impression that the pastor has pored hours over his books in the study. "You should . . . you should . . . you should . . . ! But don't ever . . . or . . . !"

And so, week after week, God's children go home with spiritual blisters on their toes, feeling good after their weekly discipline, for their guilt feelings have once again been aroused showing them how weak they are in the faith, fulfilling their emotional "need" of protestant asceticism.

On the other hand, however, we find the "doctrine hounds." In such a setting, the message would never be complete without seven or eight participles being parsed from the Greek language, a couple of Hebrew word pictures, quotations from Keil and Delitzsch, and a complete grammatical analysis.

Never a word is uttered concerning how all of this relates to the needs of the contemporary Christian family, what it really means to the life pattern of the twentieth-century teenager, or what response should be evoked from such knowledge. And sure enough, week by week, the children of God leave their assembly place exclaiming to one another, "Boy, that sure was *deep* today," but always returning the following Sunday with the same spiritual stature with which they left the week before.

Once again, we ask the question:

WHAT DID JESUS DO?

And beginning at Moses and all the prophets, he expounded unto them in all the scriptures . . . And they said one to another, Did not our heart burn within us, while he talked with us by [along] the way, and while he opened to us the scriptures? Then opened he their understanding, that they might understand the scriptures (Luke 24:27, 32, 45; AV).

And Jesus came up and spoke to them, saying . . . Go therefore and make disciples . . . teaching them to observe all that I commanded you . . . (Matthew 28:18-20).

FURTHER BIBLICAL INSTRUCTION

A few years later at Miletus, the Apostle Paul gave his farewell address to the pastors of the Ephesian church who came there to meet him. He told them:

For I have not shunned to declare unto you all the counsel of God. Take heed therefore unto yourselves, and to all the flock, over which the Holy Ghost [Spirit] hath made you overseers, to feed the church of God, which he hath purchased with his own blood (Acts 20:27,28; AV).

SIGNIFICANT OBSERVATIONS

Notice carefully the ministry of our Lord. Four significant observations may be made concerning His methodology in the Luke 24 passage: (1) "He expounded unto them." He did not merely quote a few verses to them coupled with a clever poem and a joke. Neither did He spiritualize a Bible story by finding a symbol in every strap of a man's sandal. He didn't have to take any extreme action to get them prepared emotionally. He *expounded* the Scriptures. He exposed to them what the Scriptures were actually saying.

(2) He expounded unto them, "in all the scriptures." In Jesus' day there existed only the Old Testament, which

consisted of three sections: the Law, the Prophets, and the Writings. Verse 44 specifically mentions that Jesus in His exposition expounded from each of these three sections. He did not withhold any portion of the Scriptures from His disciples, but expounded from *all*.

(3) His exposition evoked an immediate response: "And they said one to another, Did not our heart burn within us, while he talked with us by [along] the way, and while he opened to us the scriptures?" His ministry affected their lives. The very nature of His accurate handling of the Scriptures automatically and spontaneously effected the response.

(4) "Opened he their understanding, that they might understand the scriptures." He not only taught them what the Scriptures *say* but He accurately interpreted for them what the Scriptures *mean*. And we know from the ministry of Jesus recorded in all four Gospels that He not only explained the Scriptures, but He also illustrated their meaning with parables and object lessons.

Yes, Jesus' ministry was both didactic *and* sermonic. He taught them biblical doctrine from every portion of the Scriptures—systematic biblical doctrine, accurate biblical doctrine—but He did not stop there. He applied it to their lives as well!

Robert Traina writes that the first three steps of genuine inductive Bible study are observation, interpretation, and application.[1] Biblical preaching is really nothing more than public Bible study. If it is not, does the pastor think that he can accomplish more with his own words than with the words of God? And if biblical preaching is public Bible study, then these three ingredients should all be present. The balanced pulpit will declare what the Bible says, what the Bible means, and what the Bible means to people today.

Haddon W. Robinson, Chairman of the Department of Pastoral Ministries at Dallas Theological Seminary, says:

> I believe that the type of preaching which most effectively lays open the Bible so that people are confronted by its truth is expository preaching. At its best, expository preaching is "the presentation of biblical truth, derived from and transmitted through a historical, grammatical and spirit-guided study of a passage in its context, which the Holy Spirit applies first to the life of the preacher and then through him to his congregation."[2]

PUTTING IT ALL TOGETHER

In light of the discussion above, it is expedient to consider five homiletical dangers which threaten a balanced pulpit.

The Danger of Riding Hobbies

Many preachers seem to have a pet doctrine which they manage to include in every message they preach—soul-winning, baptism, election, prophecy, sanctification, social ethics, the Holy Spirit, separation, prayer, sovereignty, etc. Each of these doctrines is important but should never be dwelt on at the expense of the rest of the Word of God.

A friend of mine saw "soul-winning" in every verse of the Bible. Granted, his people knew well how to win souls but that was just about the extent of their spiritual experience and biblical knowledge! It would be well for each preacher periodically to take an objective look at the doctrinal diet he is feeding his people, and assess it in the light of the *principle of totality.*

Second Timothy 3:16 says, "All scripture is given by inspiration of God, and is profitable for doctrine, for reproof, for correction, for instruction in righteousness" (AV). The theology in Habakkuk is too precious to be ignored! Today's teenager needs the message of Ecclesiastes! Every book in the Bible was deliberately written for our benefit and divinely included for our spiritual maturity. Every chapter was included for our benefit. *Every verse* was God-breathed just for us so that we might have a *complete* revelation from God. There are just too many truths in the Bible that impel us never to hang on to only a few. The balanced pulpit declares the *whole* counsel of God.

And it is the whole counsel that edifies the whole man. Koller writes:

> The presentation of theological truth must be comprehensive enough to illumine the mind, to stir the emotion, to move the will, to win the whole man—"heart, soul, mind, strength" (Mark 12:30).[3]

The Danger of "Storyitis"

To eat three times a day is not only normal but necessary. However, if a person begins to eat five and six full-course meals a day, it is time for him to see a physician. Stories are not only normal in the pulpit, they are necessary. Jesus Himself used parables. But if Jesus always and only spoke in parables, we would be of all men most miserable! He merely used parables to illustrate His doctrine.

A preacher is not a storyteller—he is a Bible expositor. Donald Grey Barnhouse once said, "Expository preaching is the art of explaining the text of the Word of God, using all the experiences of life and learning to illuminate the exposition."⁴

The preacher's stories are to illustrate the doctrine, not vice versa. There may be some people who like a little coffee in their cream, but most of us prefer it the other way around. This is a pit that is very easy to fall into. To give a half hour of stories can save a lot of time in the study and will even guarantee some hearty handshakes in the vestibule. However, we ought then to face the fact that for the most part, we are responsible for the spiritual retardation and malnutrition of our people.

Paul told Timothy all *Scripture* was profitable. That is why he also told Timothy to "study to shew thyself approved unto God, a workman that needeth not to be ashamed, rightly dividing the word of truth" (2 Timothy 2:15, AV).

Timothy was taught the *principle of exegesis.* He was to equip himself to accurately bring out the actual meaning of every word of God. This means hard work for the preacher. It is not the normal work of the Holy Spirit divinely, mystically and instantaneously to give the preacher an immediate understanding of the true meaning of a verse of Scripture. It takes a little work . . . a little digging . . . a little observation . . . a little research.

First Thessalonians 5:26 will never be fully understood without a knowledge of the cultural context. Psalm 51:11 will be a very confusing verse without a knowledge of dispensationalism. Acts 2:38 will be a doctrinal stumbling block without some knowledge of Greek. First John 3:3 can turn into a false promise without an understanding of grammar. First John 3:9 will look very perplexing to someone without a knowledge of Johannine theology. Acts 8:14-17 would throw a monkey wrench into pneumatology without an awareness of the historical background of the passage.

There is no shortcut to true biblical expository preaching. The preacher must be willing to pay the price. The Holy Spirit will not do his work for him. Rather, the Holy Spirit has given the pastor the responsibility to "study" to show himself as an approved workman. A loving preacher will not flash his knowledge of Hebrew, Greek, and theology for the sake of impressing his congregation, but he will earnestly study these areas in his office in order to explain the Scriptures accurately to his people.

The Danger of Non-Variation

In terms of pedagogy, the worst method is the overused method. Still using the same principles of exposition, Jesus Christ frequently varied His pedagogical methods. Sometimes He used audio-visuals. Sometimes He did not. Sometimes He taught His disciples topically. Other times, He taught them textually.

It is also wise for today's preacher to exercise creativity and variation in his preaching. While maintaining the principles of observation, interpretation, and application, the speaker still has countless opportunities of variation in getting across the message of God effectively. He can present a topical message, a textual message, a synthetic message, a biographical message, an historical message.

One of the many reasons Pastor Wiersbe compiled the *Treasury of the World's Great Sermons* was to demonstrate variety in good preaching.[5] The preacher can use drama, audio-visuals, handouts, outlined bulletin inserts, role play, etc. This helps immensely to keep your people excited about God's Word.

The Danger of Impersonal Oratory

Several years ago, I became acquainted with a preacher whose accent changed as soon as he hit the pulpit. Before the service, he had an ordinary midwestern accent. As soon as he began preaching, however, he instantly acquired a beautiful British accent. Whether he, himself, was aware of it or not, I do not know. It was certainly something to hear. Another young pastor with whom I enjoyed frequent fellowship would always lower his voice greatly behind the pulpit. He sounded twenty years older every time he preached.

In both these situations the messages came across as being very impersonal. They both exhibited fine oratory—but it would fit much better in a public forum than among the body of believers.

Almost seventy years ago William Evans warned his preacher friends:

> Many a man has failed in his ministry, when otherwise he would have been a glorious success, simply because he was not willing to take himself as God made him. The very individuality with which God has endowed us is the very thing which makes us worth hearing—otherwise a graphophone could do the work about as well and at less expense.

> It is worthy of note that men who copy the ways and manners of other preachers who have been successful almost always copy their faults and not their virtues, and in the attempt to do so become ridiculous in the extreme.[6]

The pastor must not only be himself when he is in the

homes of his people; he must be himself behind the pulpit as well if he is to communicate realistically and effectively the Word of God.

This is not to say that his message must sound as personal as a private conversation over coffee. Obviously, if he is to be heard and understood by all the people, he must intensify his volume, exaggerate his enunciation, and amplify his gestures. This is not role playing, but rather giving a courtesy to the congregation.

I once heard a preacher who believed that it was role playing to project his voice and incorporate the principles of public speaking. He merely wanted to "share from his heart." Within five minutes almost everyone around me was asleep! He certainly did not captivate our attention!

If it is wrong for a preacher to be concerned with the principles of public speaking, then it is equally unspiritual for a musician to practice and project. Obviously, such reasoning is absurd. We must strive for excellence and effectiveness in public communication. A sincere heart before God and man remains the criterion for validity in the oral art of preaching. It is never wrong to amplify one's personality in order to communicate. What we need to watch is the impersonation of a personality that simply isn't ours.

The Danger of Abstract Application

This danger is quite subtle. Simply stated, an abstract application is a very general word of exhortation at the end of a message, without giving any specific instruction. For an example, a man might preach on Acts 1:8 and then at the end of the message apply the verse by saying, "This verse should challenge each of us to be a witness—Amen." They already assumed that! *How* should they witness? What specific steps should they take in light of this principle?

An application is to be *specific.* It should not only tell them *what* to do but *how* to do it! How does a child put it into practice, a teenager, an adult, a housewife? What specific course of action should be taken in light of a message before God? In the home? In one's emotional life? At the factory? In the classroom?

James 1:22 tells believers, "But be ye doers of the word, and not hearers only, deceiving your own selves" (AV). One of the responsibilities of the preacher is to tell the congregation lovingly *how* to be a doer of the Word.

Application is therefore not merely specific, but immediate. Baumann asserts:

> Application is also *present tense.* It is not simply, What shall we do? but, What shall we do now? The gospel is specifically related to the audience at hand. Only rarely should the application be future tense.[7]

Obviously, the application must be consistent with the intended meaning of the text. Walter Rhodes warns against causing a scriptural text to be "alienated from its true meaning and applied to a peculiar or local condition. It is not wise to alter the meaning of a text simply to fit a singular need . . ."[8]

Yet on the other hand, the preacher is obligated by virtue of his very calling to make specific application that *is* consistent with the exposition. Broadus, the prince of homileticians, strongly affirms:

> To interpret and apply his text in accordance with the real meaning is one of the preacher's most sacred duties. He stands before the people for the very pur-

pose of teaching and exhorting them out of the Word of God.[9]

The first step is to become application-conscious. Preaching for results ought to be the perpetual goal. One way to keep this mind-set is to list specific objectives that you are trying to accomplish in the hearer as a result of the sermon or series of sermons. Both general and specific objectives should be considered.

For example, let's say for the next seven weeks you plan to preach a series of sermons on the doctrine of God from seven great passages. Three general objectives might be stated in this fashion: (1) The hearer will be able to describe the nature and character of God. (2) The hearer will be able to recognize the relationship between the doctrine of God and his own personal life. (3) The hearer will be able to apply learned biblical truths to his life in beginning a process of behavioral change.

Three specific objectives might be: (1) The hearer will be able to give a clear witness to his relationship with God. (2) The hearer will be able to establish a meaningful prayer life. (3) The hearer will be able to rid himself of specific areas of doubt and replace them with confident trust.

These specific objectives would be even more specifically delineated as the preacher seeks to apply the "how to" aspect according to the unique situations of his own congregation. At any rate, application *must* be in focus. Preaching must be for results or it ceases to be preaching. Information must bring insight. Insight changes attitudes. Attitudes produce action. But good preaching facilitates all four.

In summary, then, the balanced preacher is one who teaches doctrine and gives application. He is one who both instructs and exhorts. He gives the whole counsel of God from the entire spectrum of biblical truth. He studies diligently in order that he may expound the words of Scripture accurately. He varies the style of his message in order to stay fresh in his approach to the Word of God. He speaks to the congregation realistically, not with artificial oratory. He makes the application specific and zeroes right in on where his people live. These are the marks of the pulpit in the balanced Christian church.

PUTTING IT INTO PARAPHRASE

And beginning with the law and the prophets, He expounded to them scripture from the entire spectrum of biblical revelation. And they said to each other, Were you as challenged as I was when He explained those scriptures? . . . Then He interpreted the scriptures to them, in order that they might clearly understand their meaning (Luke 24:27,32,45).

APPLICATION PROJECT

For the Preacher

1. One of the best ways to establish a "balanced pulpit" is the development of an annual preaching calendar. Obviously you will want to leave yourself open for change into which God's Spirit may guide you, but such a plan of predetermined direction is essential to a balanced preaching ministry.

2. Sit down and develop your own preaching calendar if you have not already done so. Follow these four basic steps:

   a. List your general aims for the upcoming year. As an example, here is a list of the general aims I've set for my ministry in the year ahead:

      1) To attempt a balance between the Old Testament and the New Testament.
      2) To attempt a balance between doctrine and practical living.
      3) To emphasize the personal nature of Christianity.
      4) To touch upon areas of major interest.
      5) To touch upon areas of need.
      6) To preach through the type of calendar that would lend itself to evangelism.
      7) To vary the approach through biographical, historical, textual, topical, expository and dramatic exposition.
      8) To recognize special holidays of the church.
      9) To integrate special programs and conferences.

10) To avoid hobbies by attempting doctrinal balance.
11) To employ the use of interesting titles.
12) To keep the series short—especially on Sundays.

b. List your specific objectives for the year ahead. Again as an example, here are the ones I listed. By the end of the year, the faithful attender:

1) Will be able to measurably improve his/her marriage relationship or marital preparation in the case of singles.
2) Will be able to identify the fruit of the Spirit and take personal inventory of his/her own spiritual growth.
3) Will be able to meet difficulties and disappointments with a stronger spiritual stamina and understanding.
4) Will be able to perceive the marks of a healthy church and thus be able to make a more qualitative contribution to the church himself.
5) Will have an appreciation of the lives of biblical characters and draw points of similarities of life experience in personal application.
6) Will know how to lead someone to Christ.
7) Will be able to have a greater worshipful appreciation of the Three Persons of the Godhead.
8) Will be able to state the biblical answers to commonly asked crucial questions.
9) Will be able to begin or improve his/her prayer

        life.

10) Will be able to deal with life's greatest problems without being overcome by emotional stress.

11) Will be doctrinally conversant.

12) Will be challenged to a life of zeal for God in the context of grace.

c. With a calendar in hand, prepare a format of series that will facilitate the above aims and objectives, giving the dates, general texts, and creative titles. Include Sunday mornings, Sunday evenings and Wednesday evenings. Take into consideration the special activities of the church which have already been scheduled as well as Christian holidays. For example:

1) Sunday mornings:

6/4-6/11	"The Shepherd and His Sheep" (Epistles)
6/18-7/30	"Life is a Family Affair" (Genesis)
8/20-10/1	"Our Lord's Living Letters" (Revelation)
10/22-11/12	"Getting to Know God" (Topical)
11/26-12/24	"A Look at the *Living* Word" (Topical)
1/7-2/4	"Meeting the Third Person" (Topical)
2/18-3/18	"Words of a Weeping Prophet" (Lamentations)
4/8-6/3	"Glimpses of Grace" (2 Corin thians)

2) Sunday evenings:

6/4-7/30	"The Fruit of the Spirit" (Galatians)
8/20-10/1	"Walking with the Saints" (Biographical)
10/22-11/12	"God's Sovereignty and Man" (Jonah)
1/7-2/4	"Faith's Walking Shoes" (James)
2/18-3/18	"Life's Greatest Problems" (Topical)
4/8-5/6	"Looking at the Future" (1 & 2 Thessalonians)
5/13-6/10	"Stories of Great Christians" (Exp. drama)

3) Wednesday evenings:

6/4-10/1	"The Discovery of Joy" (Philippians)
10/22-11/12	"The Bible Says That?" (Topical)
11/26-2/4	"Great Prayers of the Bible" (Topical)
2/18-5/6	"Traveling with the Twelve" (Gospels)
5/13-6/10	"Great Bible Themes" (Theology)

d. Next, select a passage and creative title for each message. Coordinate the messages with the series dates you have selected. Leave unassigned dates open, or plan singular messages. Keep holiday preaching in mind.

IS MY CHURCH WHAT GOD MEANT IT TO BE?

For the Layperson

1. Learn to listen to sermons intelligently. One way to do this is to take notes during the message.
2. During the message, list the following items on paper:
   a. What is the central passage?
   b. What is the big idea the preacher is trying to get across?
   c. How is he developing that idea? (List the major supporting points.)
   d. Does his idea fit the point of the passage?
   e. Which illustration made the meaning clear to you?
   f. What specific action can you or must you do in light of this message?
3. Keep a file of notes you have taken. You will be able to reuse them in your own personal study, devotional life or ministry.
4. Have dialogue with your preacher over that point which particularly struck your interest. Discussing it will even deepen its impression upon you.
5. Establish objectives in listening to sermons. What do you want to glean from your pastor's ministry?
6. Encourage your preacher by prayer and verbal appreciation.

CONCLUSION

In an evangelical world rent with extremism, the church that will most effectively minister to the believer and proclaim God's message to the unbeliever is the church with a desire for biblical balance. It will strive for a balanced purpose, a balanced program, a balanced congregation, balanced individuals, a balanced pastor, and a balanced pulpit.

The church with *perfect* balance will not exist until it is in heaven. We have been dealing in this manual with ideals. The best that we can hope for as we minister in the context of a fallen race is an awareness of the need for balance, a strong desire for balance, and a never-ending process of working toward that balance.

If you are a part of a Bible-believing church which lacks balance, do not use this book as an excuse to leave that church. The grass is only greener on the other side of the fence until you get there. You can be the catalyst to begin the process of balance in your church. Share these principles with the leadership, pray for wisdom, and strive for balance in your own life.

Engaged in a spiritual process, Christian determination must always bear the ingredient of patience. May God grant us both.

NOTES

Introduction: The Stained Glass Pendulum

1. Paul R. Jackson, *The Doctrine and Administration of the Church* (Des Plaines, IL: Regular Baptist Press, 1968), p. 27.

1. Balancing the Purpose

1. Alvin J. Lindgren, *Foundations for Purposeful Church Administration* (New York: Abingdon Press, 1965), p. 23.

2. Philip R. Williams, "Grammar Notes on the Noun and the Verb" (unpublished class notes, 203 Greek Grammar and Syntax, Dallas Theological Seminary, August, 1971), p. 36.

3. Lloyd Merle Perry and Edward John Lias, *A Manual of Pastoral Problems and Procedures* (Grand Rapids: Baker House, 1962), p. iv.

2. Balancing the Program

3. Balancing the People

1. J. A. Hadfield, *Childhood and Adolescence* (Baltimore: Penguin Books, Inc., 1962), p. 25.

2. W. Stanley Mooneyham, "Ministering to the Hunger Belt," *Christianity Today* (January 3, 1975), p. 10.

3. Erich Fromm, *The Art of Loving* (New York: Harper and Row Publishers, 1956), p. 22.

4. Henry Drummond, *The Greatest Thing in the World* (Kansas City: Hallmark Cards, 1967), p. 13.

5. Drummond, *The Greatest Thing in the World,* p. 13.

6. John Lewis Beatty and Oliver A. Johnson, eds., *Heritage of Western Civilization* (Englewood Cliffs, NJ: Prentice Hall, 1971), p. 397.

7. Gary Hauck, "Satan's Secret Weapons Against the Young Pastor," *Baptist Bulletin* Vol. 42 (July/August, 1976), p. 16.

8. Hadfield, *Childhood and Adolescence,* p. 256.

9. Francis A. Schaeffer, *The Church at the End of the 20th Century* (Downers Grove, IL: Intervarsity Press, 1970), pp. 147-8.

10. Ray Stedman, *Body Life* (Glendale, CA: G/L Publications, Regal Books, 1972), p. 107.

11. Stedman, *Body Life,* p. 110-1.

12. Schaeffer, *The Church at the End of the 20th Century,* pp. 143-4.

13. Stedman, *Body Life,* p. 51.

14. Lawrence O. Richards, *A New Face for the Church* (Grand Rapids: Zondervan Publishing House, 1970), p. 99.

15. Edward T. Hiscox, *The New Directory for Baptist Churches* (Grand Rapids: Kregel Publications, 1970), p. 556.

16. Richards, *A New Face for the Church,* p. 101.

17. Robert G. Gromacki, *The Modern Tongues Movement* (Philadelphia: Presbyterian and Reformed Publishing Co., 1967), p.

126.

18. Gene A. Getz, *The Measure of a Man* (Glendale, CA: G/L Publications, Regal Books, 1974), p. 17.

19. Getz, *The Measure of a Man,* p. 17.

20. Gene A. Getz, *Sharpening the Focus of the Church* (Chicago: Moody Press, 1974), pp. 112-4.

21. Getz, *Sharpening the Focus of the Church,* p. 116.

22. Getz, *Sharpening the Focus of the Church,* p. 117.

4. Balancing the Person

1. Kenneth O. Gangel, "Foundations for the Christian College, From Harvard to HEW," *Bibliotheca Sacra* Vol. 435, No. 537 (January-March, 1978), p. 10.

2. Gerald L. Hershey and James O. Lugo, *Living Psychology* (London: The Macmillian Company, 1970), p. 353.

3. Howard J. Clinebell, Jr., *The Mental Health Ministry of the Local Church* (Nashville: Abingdon Press, 1965), p. 13.

4. S. I. McMillen, *None of These Diseases* (Old Tappan, NJ: Fleming H. Revell Company, 1963), pp. 9-75.

5. C. S. Lovett, *Jesus Wants You Well* (Baldwin Park, CA: Personal Christianity, 1973), pp. 135-76.

6. Lovett, *Jesus Wants You Well,* p. 232.

7. Marion H. Nelson, *Why Christians Crack Up* (Chicago: Moody Press, 1967), p. 61.

8. Paul D. Meier, *Christian Child-Rearing and Personality Development* (Grand Rapids: Baker Book House, 1977), p. 26.

9. Meier, *Christian Child-Rearing and Personality Development*, p. 26.

10. Meier, *Christian Child-Rearing and Personality Development*, p. 27.

11. Frank Minirth, *Christian Psychiatry* (Old Tappan, NJ: Fleming H. Revell Company, 1977), pp. 121-4.

12. Lovett, *Jesus Wants You Well*, p. 233.

13. *Diagnostic and Statistical Manual of Mental Disorders*, 2nd ed. (Washington, D.C.: American Psychiatric Association, 1968), p. 43.

14. Richard Quebedeaux, *The Young Evangelicals* (New York: Harper & Row, 1974), pp. 101-2.

15. Paul R. Jackson, *The Doctrine and Administration of the Church* (Des Plaines, IL: Regular Baptist Press, 1969), p. 83.

16. Robert P. Lightner, *Neo-Evangelicalism* (Des Plaines, IL: Regular Baptist Press, 1965), p. 152.

17. Charles Caldwell Ryrie, *Balancing the Christian Life* (Chicago: Moody Press, 1969), p. 66.

18. Ryrie, *Balancing the Christian Life,* p. 67.

5. Balancing the Pastor

1. Lawrence Frederic Shaffer and Edward Joseph Shoben, Jr., *The Psychology of Adjustment* (Boston: Houghton Mifflin Company, 1956), p. 168.

2. Shaffer and Shoben, *The Psychology of Adjustment,* pp. 176-7.

3. Howard F. Sugden and Warren W. Wiersbe, *Confident Pastoral Leadership* (Chicago: Moody Press, 1977), p. 30.

4. Gary Hauck, "Satan's Secret Weapons Against the Young Pastor," *Baptist Bulletin* Vol. 42, No. 2 (July-August, 1976), pp. 16, 47.

5. Charles Haddon Spurgeon, *Lectures to My Students* (Grand Rapids: Associated Publishers and Authors, 1971), p. 148.

6. John Louis Beatty and Oliver A. Johnson, eds., *Heritage of Western Civilization* (Englewood Cliffs, NJ: Prentice Hall, 1958), p. 2:331.

7. Beatty and Johnson, *Heritage of Western Civilization,* p. 2:251.

8. Gene A. Getz, *The Measure of A Man* (Glendale, CA: G/L Publications, Regal Books, 1978), pp. 24-5.

6. Balancing the Pulpit

1. Robert A. Traina, *Methodical Bible Study* (Wilmore, Ken: Asbury Theological Seminary, 1952), pp. 1-228.

2. Haddon W. Robinson, "Preaching with an Impact," *Good News Broadcaster* Vol. 35, No. 11 (December, 1977), pp. 31-2.

3. Charles W. Koller, *Expository Preaching Without Notes* (Grand Rapids: Baker Book House, 1961), pp. 108-9.

4. Clarence Stonelynn Roddy, ed., *We Prepare and We Preach* (Chicago: Moody Press, 1959), p. 29.

5. Warren W. Wiersbe, *Treasury of the World's Great Sermons* (Grand Rapids: Kregel Publications, 1977), p. ix.

6. William Evans, *How to Prepare Sermons and Gospel Addresses* (Chicago: The Bible Institute Colportage Association, 1913), p. 18.

7. J. Daniel Baumann, *An Introduction to Contemporary Preaching* (Grand Rapids: Baker Book House, 1972), p. 244.

8. Walter Rhodes, *Homiletics and Preaching* (Baltimore: The Peters Publishing and Printing Co., 1906), p. 40.

9. John A. Broadus, *On the Preparation and Delivery of Sermons* (New York: Harper & Row, Publishers, 1944), p. 24.

BIBLIOGRAPHY

Adams, Jay E., *The Christian Counseling Manual* (Philadelphia: Presbyterian and Reformed Publishing Company, 1977)

Armerding, Hudson T., *Christianity and the World of Thought* (Chicago: Moody Press, 1963)

Baumann, J. Daniel, *An Introduction to Contemporary Preaching* (Grand Rapids: Baker Book House, 1972)

Baxter, Richard, *The Reformed Pastor* (Edinburgh: The Banner of Truth Trust, 1974)

Beatty, John Lewis and Oliver A. Johnson, eds., *Heritage of Western Civilization*. 2 vols. (Englewood Cliffs, NJ: Prentice Hall, 1971)

Benson, Clarence H., *Understanding Children and Youth* (Wheaton, IL: Evangelical Teacher Training Association, 1969)

Broadus, John A., *On the Preparation and Delivery of Sermons* (New York: Harper & Row, 1944)

Clinebell, Howard J. Jr., *The Mental Health Ministry of the Local Church* (Nashville: Abingdon Press, 1965)

Clinebell, Howard J. and Charlotte H., *The Intimate Marriage* (New York: Harper & Row, 1970)

Coleman, Robert E., *The Master Plan of Evangelism* (Westwood: Fleming H. Revell Company, 1964)

Collins, Gary, *Search for Reality* (Wheaton: Key Publishers, 1969)

Crabb, Lawrence J., *Effective Biblical Counseling* (Grand Rapids: Zondervan Publishing House, 1977)

Crane, William E., *Where God Comes In* (Waco: Word Books, 1970)

Drummond, Henry, *The Greatest Thing in the World* (Kansas City: Hallmark Incorporated, 1967)

Evans, William, *How To Prepare Sermons and Gospel Addresses* (Chicago: The Bible Institute Colportage Association, 1913)

Ferre, Nels F. S., "Contemporary Theology in the Light of 100 Years," *Theology Today*. Vol. 15 (October, 1958)

Fromm, Erich, *The Art of Loving* (New York: Harper & Row, 1956)

Gangel, Kenneth O., *Leadership for Church Leadership* (Chicago: Moody Press, 1970)

Getz, Gene A., *The Measure of a Church* (Glendale, CA: G/L Regal Books, 1975)

Getz, Gene A., *The Measure of a Man* (Glendale, CA: G/L Regal Books, 1974)

Getz, Gene A., *Sharpening the Focus of the Church* (Chicago: Moody Press, 1974)

Gromacki, Robert G., *The Modern·Tongues Movement* (Presbyterian and Reformed Publishing Company, 1967)

Hadfield, J. A., *Childhood and Adolescence* (Baltimore: Penguin Books Inc., 1962)

Hauck, Gary, "Satan's Secret Weapons Against the Young Pastor," *The Baptist Bulletin* Vol. 42, No. 2, (July/August, 1976, pp. 16, 47)

Hendricks, Howard G., *Heaven Help the Home* (Wheaton: Victor Books, 1973

Hershey, Gerald L. and James O. Lugo, *Living Psychology* (London: The Macmillan Company, 1970)

Henry, Carl F. H., *Evangelical Responsibility in Contemporary Theology* (Grand Rapids: Wm. B. Eerdmans Pub. Co., 1957)

Henry, Carl F. H., *A Plea for Evangelical Demonstration* (Grand Rapids: Baker Book House, 1971)

Hirsh, Herbert L., *The Winning of the Lost* (Published by the author: 415 N. E. 147th Terrace, Miami, Florida 33161, n.d.)

I.F.C.A. Church Handbook (Wheaton. IL: Independent Fundamental Churches of America, 1969)

Jackson, Paul R., *The Doctrine and Administration of the Church* (Des Plaines, IL: Regular Baptist Press, 1970)

Kennedy, D. James, *Evangelism Explosion* (Wheaton: Tyndale House Publishers, 1970)

Kilinski, Kenneth K. and Jerry C. Wofford, *Organization and Leadership in the Local Church* (Grand Rapids: Zondervan Publishing House, 1973)

Koller, Charles W., *Expository Preaching Without Notes* (Grand Rapids: Baker Book House, 1962)

Lightner, Robert Paul, *Neo-Evangelicalism* (Des Plaines: Regular Baptist Press, 1965)

Lightner, Robert Paul, *Neo-Liberalism* (Chicago: Regular Baptist Press, 1959)

Little, Paul E., *How To Give Away Your Faith* (Downers Grove: Inter-Varsity Press, 1977)

Lovett, C. S., *Jesus Wants You Well* (Baldwin Park, CA: Personal Christianity, 1973)

Mace, David R., *Getting Ready For Marriage* (Nashville: Abingdon Press, 1972)

McMillen, S. I., *None of These Diseases* (Old Tappan, NJ: Fleming H. Revell Company, 1963)

Meier, Paul D., *Christian Child-Rearing and Personality Development* (Grand Rapids: Baker Book House, 1977)

Minirth, Frank, *Christian Psychiatry* (Old Tappan, NJ: Fleming H. Revell Company, 1977)

Mooneyham, W. Stanley, "Ministering to the Hunger Belt," *Christianity Today* (3 January 1975, p. 10)

Moore, Waylon B., *New Testament Follow-Up* (Grand Rapids: Wm. B. Eerdmans Company, 1973)

Narramore, Clyde M., *Encyclopedia of Psychological Problems* (Grand Rapids: Zondervan Publishing House, 1976)

Nelson, Marion H., *Why Christians Crack Up* (Chicago: Moody Press, 1974)

Oates, Wayne E., *The Christian Pastor* (Philadelphia: The Westminster Press, 1964)

Perry, Lloyd Merle and Edward John Lias, *A Manual of Pastoral Problems and Procedures* (Grand Rapids: Baker Book House, 1962)

Pickering, Ernest D., *The Theology of Evangelism* (Clarks Summit, PA: Baptist Bible College Press, 1976)

Quebedeaux, Richard, *The Young Evangelicals* (New York: Harper & Row, 1974)

Rhodes, Walter, *Homiletics and Preaching* (Baltimore: The Peters Publishing and Printing Co., 1906)

Richards, Lawrence O., *A New Face for the Church* (Grand Rapids: Zondervan Publishing House, 1970)

Robinson, Haddon W., "Preach with an Impact," *Good News Broadcaster.* Vol. 35, No. 11 (December 1967, pp. 31-32)

Roddy, Clarence Stonelynn, *We Prepare and Preach* (Chicago: Moody Press, 1959)

Ryrie, Charles Caldwell, *Balancing the Christian Life* (Chicago:

Moody Press, 1969)

Schaeffer, Francis A., *The Church at the End of the 20th Century* (Downer's Grove: Intervarsity Press, 1970)

Shaffer, Laurance Frederic and Edward Joseph Shoben, Jr., *The Psychology of Adjustment* (Boston: Houghton Mifflin Company, 1956)

Spurgeon, Charles Haddon, *Lectures to My Students* (Grand Rapids: Associated Publishers and Authors, 1971)

Stedman, Ray, *Body Life* (Glendale, CA: G/L Regal Books, 1972)

Sugden, Howard F. and Warren W. Wiersbe, *Confident Pastoral Leadership* (Chicago: Moody Press, 1977)

Traina, Robert A., *Methodical Bible Study* (Published by the author, 1952)

Walvoord, John E., ed. *Christian Counseling for Contemporary Problems* (Dallas: Dallas Theological Seminary, n.d.)

Westberg, Granger E., *Minister and Doctor Meet* (New York: Harper & Row, 1961)

Wiersbe, Warren W., *Treasury of the World's Great Sermons* (Grand Rapids: Kregel Publications, 1977)

Wiersbe, Warren, *Walking with the Giants* (Grand Rapids: Baker Book House, 1976)

Winter, Gerald D. and Eugene M. Nuss, *The Young Adult* (Glenview, IL: Scott, Foresman and Company, 1969)

Wright, H. Norman, *Communication: Key to Your Marriage* (Glendale: CA: G/L Regal Publishers, 1974)

64256

DATE

3 '80

SEP 2

FEB 6 '81

'82

MAR 5

APR 7

SEP 17 1984

SEP 24 1987

SEP 1 5 1988

SEP 27 1990

OCT 1 8 1991

MAR 0 8 2004

JOSTEN'S 30 508